CONTENTS

ABOUT THE AUTHORS

Robin G. A. Bolton B.Ed.

Rob is a retired High School teacher from the West Midlands, who researches, writes and publishes upon aspects of social history, particularly those relating to the Brigade movement. With many decades of youth-work in Boys' Brigade and Marching Bands behind him he remains an active President of a Boys' Brigade Battalion, and is Chairman of the Church Lads' and Church Girls' Brigade Historical Group which manages the national archives of that organisation. Over the last few years he has been closely involved with the creation of the two Brigade Memorial gardens, BB & CLCGB, at the National Memorial Arboretum in Staffordshire. His endeavours with the gardens were partly inspired as a direct response to viewing hundreds of Brigade lads' with smiling faces looking out from pre - WW1 photographic postcards in his collection.

Leslie G. Howie M.A. (Hons) Dip. Ed.

Les, recently retired from teaching at George Watson's College in Edinburgh. He brings to this work, many years of experience in research and historical investigation including the recent compilation and publication of a comprehensive history of his school. Since collaborating with Rob for the book 'Badges of the Brigade' in 2000, he has become interested in the origins and growth of the Brigade movement, particularly The Boys' Brigade with which he has been associated for most of his life. Like Rob, Les has a history of teaching and leading youth marching bands, but of the traditional Scottish Pipe - Band variety.

Wilder than Panthers and as ignorant as the Heathens

The Origins of the British Brigade Movement
1750 - 1883

Rob Bolton and Les Howie

RB Publishing

RB Publishing

First published in 2009 by RB Publishing
116, Aldridge Road
Little Aston
Aldridge
WALSALL
WS9 0PF

© Copyright 2009 Rob Bolton & Les Howie

British Library Cataloguing-in-publication Data:
A catalogue record for this book is available from the British Library

ISBN 978-0-9521381-4-3

Design & Layout by Robin G A Bolton
Typeset in 10p Book Antiqua by
RB Publishing, Little Aston, Aldridge, Walsall

Printed and bound in Great Britain by
Warwick Printing Company Limited
Caswell Road, Leamington Spa, Warwickshire, CV31 1QD

Parts of this work were included in a paper delivered at the Durham Youth & Community Work
Conference in 2003 at Ushaw College and first published under the title 'First for Boys?' in 'Drawing on
the Past - Studies in the History of Community and Youth Work', (2006) edited by Ruth Gilchrist, Tony
Jeffs and Jean Spence published for 'Youth & Policy' by the National Youth Agency Leicester.

Other similar books from RB Publishing:
Boys of the Brigade - Volumes 1 (1991) ISBN 978-1-870708-50-0 (1993) ISBN 978-0-9521381-0-5
Badges of the Brigade - Volume 1 (2000) ISBN 978-0-9521381-1-2
Forward! The Birmingham Battalion of the Boys' Brigade 1902 - 2002 (2002) ISBN 978-0-9521381-2-9

'The idea of the Brigade is this. It is a new movement for turning out boys, instead of savages. The average boy, as you know, is a pure animal. He is not evolved; and, unless he is taken in hand by somebody who cares for him and who understands him, he will be very apt to make a mess of his life - not to speak of the lives of other people.'
Professor Henry Drummond. (1893)

<u>The Object of The Boys' Brigade:</u>
The advancement of Christ's Kingdom among Boys and the promotion of habits of Obedience, Reverence, Discipline, Self-respect, and all that tends towards a true Christian Manliness.

FOREWORD

by

The Right Honourable John Viscount Thurso MP

Thurso, Caithness, September 2009

Often I use the BB hall in Thurso for my advice clinics sitting in the museum filled with memorabilia and historic records from all over the country, among them many pictures of my father. A memory I cherish is of him, shortly after he had become President of The Boys' Brigade, composing an article aimed at the boys. He explained to me how he wanted to put his point across by linking the traditional values of the brigade - he was particularly keen on Christian manliness - with the challenges of the modern world, and how the work of the BB was both relevant and needed in the world of today. His work with the BB gave him tremendous satisfaction, indeed I think it was one of the most fulfilling tasks he ever undertook.

Yet despite all those connections I had no idea of the deep roots of the brigade movement that had existed for a long time before Sir William Smith founded the BB, nor that my 4xgreat aunt Catherine Sinclair had been so involved, nor indeed that she had founded 'The Ulbster Volunteers'. All of this fascinating history is revealed in this excellent book 'Wilder than Panthers and as ignorant as the Heathens' by Rob Bolton and Les Howie who are to be congratulated on bringing this important history together with a lively and engaging style.

2009 is the centenary of the award of Sir William Smith's knighthood. His work built on the past and was made relevant for his time. I know how much my father wanted to see the same for today's BB. A critical part of understanding how to evolve for the future lies in understanding the past. This book is essential reading for anyone attempting that task, and a great read as well.

I hope you enjoy it as much as I have.

Biographical note
John Sinclair, 3rd Viscount Thurso took his seat in the House of Lords in 1995 following the death of his father Robin Sinclair. After his automatic right to sit as a Peer in the Lords was abolished in 1999, he did not attempt to remain.
At the 2001 General Election he was elected to the House of Commons as a Liberal Democrat to represent Caithness, Sutherland and Easter Ross, thus becoming the first hereditary Peer of the United Kingdom allowed to sit in the Commons without first renouncing his title. He is known as 'John Thurso MP'

PREFACE

The year 2008 - 2009 is the 125th anniversary of the founding of The Boys' Brigade in Glasgow by William Alexander Smith whilst 2009 is the centenary of his knighthood for a remarkably successful development in youth work. Smith's Brigade was the first of its type to go 'global'. Clearly there was something very special about it. Many books have been written about the history and development of the Boys' Brigade and its many progeny, but here an attempt has been made to explain why the BB came into being. What inspired it? What were its tangled and deep-seated roots? What were its religious and social foundations?

One of the most difficult tasks in compiling this book has been the need to give some semblance of order to the various chapters. Even within chapter headings, attempting to operate within a strict chronology has provided a challenge due to seemingly innumerable branches and cross-connections which would make the 'Ragged School Tree' (see page 33) seem quite straightforward. It is not possible to see the development of the Brigade movement as a linear progression. Certainly, some of the earliest growth points can be identified, as can outstandingly influential personalities and themes. What is more difficult is trying to see why similar solutions were found to what, on the face of it, seem to be entirely different questions. The transmission and promulgation of ideas is always one of the most difficult trails to follow, rife with speculation and false avenues.

The concept of a Christian 'Brigade' of boys may seem straightforward, but over time, language changes. What constitutes a 'boy' may be subject to interpretation. Similarly, the definition of a 'brigade' is many and varied. Thus it cannot be assumed that any juvenile organisation given the formal title 'Brigade' - is one. It is necessary to seek out those which conform, structurally or socially with the definition of what a 'Brigade should be, viz:

- *Boys would be aged between eight and eighteen years.*

- *There would be official 'membership' which would be voluntary and usually requiring adherence to rules, one of which would be a small membership fee.*

- *Boys would be formed into hierarchical structured groups, run by adults with varying degrees of member participation in the organisation.*

- *Uniforms or uniform accoutrements would normally be worn.*

- *Marching or some type of military drill would take place.*

- *Christianity would be taught, charity and religious observance encouraged.*

- *'Manly' physical activities would be encouraged.*

- *Christian role models for the boys' future would be presented.*

- *Elements of recreation and fun would be standard.*

- *The organisation would provide a bridge between childhood and manhood.*

- *The above would operate in such a way as to generate a feeling of 'esprit de corps' within the group in order to give the boy an understanding of his place as part of 'society' as a whole.*

Naturally, some 'Brigades' emphasised one or more of the above, whilst others introduced particular unique elements into their programmes, such as abstinence or temperance, rifle shooting, seamanship, or work skills such as bootblacking, or message carrying.

CHAPTER ONE

Introduction

Most histories and commentaries upon the 'Brigade Movement' commence in 1883 with the founding of the Boys' Brigade in Glasgow by William A. Smith. They tend to portray it as a typical late nineteenth century institution from which developed the Boy Scouts and modern Youth Service. However, was Smith's phenomenally successful Boys' Brigade a starting point, or merely a stage in the development of a movement born more than a century earlier? Organisations which predated the Boys' Brigade and probably influenced its formation will be examined in detail.

The brigade movement, particularly in the late nineteenth century, was largely composed of what we would certainly today call 'adolescents', 'young men' or even adults. The age of first entry to the Boys' Brigade and Church Lads' Brigade was twelve years. However, during this period the average age of members was seventeen years, a high percentage being discharged only upon reaching the maximum age of twenty-one. 'Industrial brigades' which continued into the early twentieth century, such as the Gordon Boys' Brigades [A] and House Boys' Brigades [B], catered exclusively for 'working boys' who left school at thirteen. References made to 'children' or 'pre-adolescents' in Brigades before 1950 are, perhaps today, unfortunate if not thoroughly misleading.[1] This older age profile did not initially apply to the various scouting organizations developed after 1908 [C] and it still remains one of the historical distinctions in the development of uniformed youth groups. Also many early Scouting organizations, such as the Incorporated Church Scout Patrols (Church of England) or Life-Saving Scouts (Salvation Army), were completely tied to particular denominations and specifically aimed at pre-adolescents.

Traditionally, and paradoxically, there has always been a clear distinction made between the movements that grew from pure philanthropy and those born of the piety of the Sunday School movement, such as that between the Glasgow Foundry Boys' Religious Society, founded in 1865, and non-Sunday school organizations such as the Shoe-black and Industrial Brigades. This dichotomy, epitomized by writers such as Checkland, [2] [D] sometimes appears less than helpful. For instance, in the early part of the 19th century the recipients of the various forms of 'brigade' work originated in one class, but their leaders, all came from another. Can it be assumed that in Glasgow those boys, rough moulders' assistants - a *'by-word for hooliganism and profanity'* - who formed the nucleus of Mary Ann Clough's original Foundry Boys' Society [E] were much different from the 'Street Arabs' rescued by William Quarrier [F] or

Dr Barnardo? Certainly the workers in most societies were motivated by religious conviction. In Scotland generally, it is unlikely that David Harris of Edinburgh, Sheriff Watson of Aberdeen, or Rev. Dr. Guthrie [G] were less pious Christian men than Alexander Mackeith [H] or William Smith.

'First for Boys' is a slogan frequently associated with The Boys' Brigade and one long used in its publicity. Perhaps the epithet is quite correct if we look at the uniformed youth organizations that have survived to the present. However, the claim implicit in the slogan is one disputed by the Army Cadet Force which claims a formation date some twenty-three years earlier. [3] Significantly, more recent Cadet histories have identified an even earlier history for the Naval Cadets.[4] These suggest that the Whitstable Lads' Brigade founded in 1856 by sailors returning from the Crimean War was a forerunner of the Sea Cadet Corps. The Whitstable Brigade is said to have been established as a result of *'concern about the apparent laziness and degradation of the youth on the streets'*. Moreover, the first uniforms were said to be typical Victorian band uniforms. [5] Thus, when is a 'Lads' Brigade' a 'Brigade' and when is it a 'Cadet Corps'? The distinction between the two becomes not only interesting, but also somewhat unclear when the origins of the movements are explored. In the early 20th century the question did not arise as many Brigade companies, even complete brigades, re-invented themselves as military cadets. [I]

As early as 1772, the 'Marine Society', founded by the philanthropist Jonas Hanway in 1756, provided a ship which was a *'sort of Dr Barnardo's Home for waifs and strays'*.[6] Marine Society boys were, in theory, trained for a life at sea, but in reality only around five per cent ended up aboard ships. Most were simply removed from the streets to prevent them becoming lay-abouts or vagrants. This reflected a widespread feeling abroad in the late eighteenth and early nineteenth centuries that there was a growing need for such interventions to undertake social 'rescue', guidance, training, the raising of self-esteem and the greatest Victorian aspiration of all: class elevation.

A very early organization in Glasgow, the City Mission, issued its first Annual Report in 1827.[7] Similar organizations were established soon after in Edinburgh and Dundee. The aim was 'to promote the spiritual welfare of the poor.' Home visits were included with eight different denominations co-operating to run it. Children were a priority, and one aim was to direct as many as possible of Glasgow's estimated 45,000 children under ten to Sabbath Schools. In 1832, 5,643 families had been visited and new classes of Religious Instruction had been established for young men and females. It was reported that 'attendance is considerable'. Clearly, a 'juvenile problem' was perceived as much then as in the 1880s.[8] Also in Glasgow, as early as 1829, a letter was sent to the Lord Provost appealing for a House of Refuge for Juvenile offenders. Boys, or 'criminals' as they were known once inside the Bridewell, came out just as they went in, amongst the same bad company. It was realized that the reasons for them being arrested were because of their appalling social conditions. Boys, '...whose vices often originate from circumstances that afford strong grounds of palliation and excuse.' Two classes of boy were determined. The first, who banded together during the day and formed gangs at night, came from worthless parents. For those boys short court sentences were not working. In fact, repeat sentences only hardened them and they became a burden on the public as paupers. A second class, however, were orphans driven out after second marriages, destitute and exposed. A refuge was seen as vital in order to break the cycle of crime and destitution and it was also requested that they should receive 'moral and religious instruction' to induce self-control and hard work, so, '... would be trained up in habits of cleanliness, regularity and order...'. [9]

By the late nineteenth century the outlook was perhaps more balanced. The need undoubtedly remained, but there was also the important matter perceived by boys' parents, namely the implanting of the desire for upward social mobility, or, at least, 'respectability'. This was certainly the case amongst many practitioners and was probably a view shared by many of its recipients, or members.[j] Perhaps it may be implied, albeit somewhat simplistically, that some organizations were launched to keep boys off the streets day and night, whilst others sought to do so only for evenings and rest days. What is truly remarkable in retrospect is the similarity of method and approach across the various Brigades and kindred organizations. Those created in the early nineteenth century to cater for the needs of the poor compare remarkably well with those established two generations later to serve the sons of the new artisan class as well as those of the lower middle-class. On the one hand, the imposition of the normative 'paternalistic' model is perhaps epitomised by the Shoe-black Brigades of the 1850s and 1860s. On the other, the full uniformed London Diocesan Church Lads' Brigade, founded in 1891, typifies an outcome of the late nineteenth century drive for 'National Efficiency'. In all, the Brigade boys were encouraged to make more of themselves, not merely for their own good, but also for the good of the nation and the empire. Reverence was instilled as a virtue and Christian Manliness portrayed as an ideal. Discipline was taught through esprit de corps, affection for the group, team games, physical and military drills, music-making, living together, sharing, and of course, the wearing of a common uniform.

In 1859, the introduction of the 'Volunteers' part-time soldiers who would, if called upon, defend the nation from the perceived threat of France, spawned a number of junior progenies. The leadership of these organizations was frequently motivated by Christian zeal, or a related endeavour such as anti-Catholicism, or temperance. National xenophobia combined with education was always going to be a winning recipe. According to The Scotsman newspaper of 26th December 1859: In Dunfermline... *'Mr Thompson, of the Commercial Academy here, in the true spirit of the volunteer movement has had a corps of from 40 to 50 boys drilled in the Music Hall, by Sergeant Kelloch, now stationed in Dunfermline, and acting as drill sergeant to the rifle corps. The present arrangements include drill twice a week, one hour each, and these in no way interfering with common scholastic exercises.'* In Aberdeen... *'the students of King's College have formed themselves into a volunteer company, and undergo drill from twelve to one o'clock daily...'* In March 1860, in Kirkcaldy, Fife, an ex-Superintendent of police, James Thompson, raised a Corps known as 'The Juvenile Volunteers'. Different sources put the age range as 10 - 17 years, or 11 - 17 years. There were initially more than 130 members which rose to 200 within a few months. This Juvenile Artillery Corps was said to be the first of its kind ever formed in Scotland. The Corps drilled in the Corn Exchange and on the sands, or in the High School playground in the summer. The smartest and tallest boys were elected as officers! Three small cannon of about two and a quarter pounds calibre were obtained for use in long-gun practice. The dress consisted of trousers with a yellow stripe, close buttoned jacket with standing collar, and a foraging cap having an orange coloured band.[10] & [11] A Cadet Corps of the London Rifle Volunteer Brigade, with 150 members aged between nine and seventeen years was active from the summer of 1860. Uniforms, which were black, were described as being *'utterly devoid of anything in the form of ornament, the stripes of the NCOs excepted.'* Black forage (pill-box) caps were worn along with black patent leather belts with a snake hook. Furnished with old Irish Constabulary Carbines, they drilled in the Guildhall on Mondays and Wednesdays between 5 and 7 p.m. with bayonet drill in the crypt. A Fife and Drum Band also operated. [12]

On February 16th 1860, The Scotsman (p4) reported a speech by Sir Archibald Alison on the Volunteer movement... *'I will go along with Lord Elcho, and say that I hope that military duties will form a part not only of the education of youth, but of children at school and that they will be taught to march, and also the manual and platoon exercises. I say this on the part of peace, for there is a Roman maxim: If you wish for peace, prepare for war.'* Lord Elcho, speaking at the Montrose

"JUST ENOUGH!"

The sentiment of the late 1880s. A young working boy is depicted in 'Sunday at Home' magazine checking his pennies to find that he has just enough to gain admission to the Magic Lantern show about the life of General Gordon.

Counties Ball, stated that the Volunteers should be a permanent institution, to exist through all time *'...and that they should train up their children to take their places in its ranks.'* [13] In November the following year, Elcho reiterated his position: *'There is a mass of evidence...it is stated by those who have much experience in the training of youth, that boys who attended drill were more docile, obedient, and prompt to do what they were told ...it does not matter what these boys are in after life, by military drill their skill in their own labour will be much more valuable, especially where they have to work together, as parts of a machine.'* He formed a committee to establish drill in schools in Scotland.[14] This is perhaps further evidence that boys were being viewed, perhaps for the first time, as having an important duty to defend their homeland as well as playing their small part in the industrial might which would secure the furtherance of the Great British Empire.

In 1862, the newly produced 'Boys Own Magazine', which was to become quite influential among young people, stated clearly its support for the Volunteer Force and recommended its young readers to take an active part:

'It is necessary that every boy, whether in town or country, should acquire a knowledge of military drill ...nothing would so much tend to promote the permanent success of the Force as to give the rising generation an interest in the doings of their fathers and elder brothers. Thus would be bred (said those who loved their country in our youth) a liking for the science of arms and the practice of athletic sports which would ultimately become a National taste, leavening the whole mass of the English nation at large.' [15]

It was a year later in 1863 before Cadets were first sanctioned in the Volunteer Regulations. Article 279 directed that cadets should be *'...boys 12 years of age and upwards, officered by gentlemen holding only honorary commissions'* [16]

It was not only the Volunteers who wished to encourage the drilling and militarisation of the young in the 1850s and 1860s. Lydia Murdoch in her study of child welfare in London between 1870 and 1914 [17] describes the influence, in the great metropolis of London, of Edward C. Tufnell the Inspector of Metropolitan Poor Law Schools between 1847 and 1874. Tufnell was very keen to employ a military system within the giant institutions created for pauper children. His great 'barrack' style children's 'homes' would, he espoused, change the children into stronger adults. Boys with 'sunken chests' who had characterised the army recruits of the Crimean campaign, he hoped would be a thing of the past.[18] Sir Edwin Chadwick, secretary of the Poor Law Board (1834-36) and social reformer, clearly supported the 'military' elements of the

Poor Law institutions. Chadwick stated that drill promoted *'sanitary'* benefits by improving the children's health and furthermore, it provided important *'moral'* benefits. *'Systematised drill'* he wrote, encouraged, *'...all that is implied in the term discipline-viz..Duty, Self-restraint, Order, Punctuality, Obedience to command, Patience.'*...drill contributed *'...to the efficiency and productive value of the pupils as labourers or as foremen in after life.'* In 1859 he argued that Britain's imperial status as an economic power, not to mention the fate of the 'Anglo Saxon Race', depended on children's military training. He claimed that the growth of the British Empire, required that civilian traders around the world should be prepared to *'clear Wilds and contend against savagery and wild beasts.'* [19]

The wearing of 'uniform' seems to us today to be one of the factors which distinguishes a 'brigade' from a 'club', although this was certainly not always so. Current opinion seems to infer that 'institutions' forced members to wear uniform as part of their method in order to help instill social control whereas the voluntary sector club or brigade employed the bribery of popular pastimes such as sports and reading rooms to achieve the same outcome. The facts, as will be outlined later, do not wholeheartedly support this hypothesis. Certainly it is the case that the uniform offered advantages to both leaders and led. Supporters of the Shoe-black Brigades in the 1850s used a uniform to make their boys acceptable to a discerning penny-paying clientele, as well as to instill a sense of personal pride and self - respect amongst members. Uniforms were also often popular with members, as they were often warmer and more comfortable than their everyday clothing. In the early years of the Glasgow Foundry Boys' Religious Society, a simple accoutrement uniform was considered to be an essential requirement for 'military drill' and drill was a very popular activity with the boys. Although shoe-black boys were given uniform tunics, caps, boots and other items of clothing they were expected to keep these clean and intact with money compulsorily deducted from their income. Many units of The Boys' Brigade operated on a similar basis with accoutrements and uniform being owned and issued by the company. This policy continued into the 20th century and remained widespread in the depressed areas up to the outbreak of the Second World War. Generous benefactors, such as the Rev. Dr. Miller founder of the St. Martin's Shoe-black Brigade in Birmingham in 1858,[20] would provide uniforms. Likewise seventy years later Mrs Barnsley, wife of the St. Martin's Boys' Brigade captain Gordon Barnsley, distributed Life-Boy jerseys (for junior boys) and collected them back in at the end of each evening meeting.[21] The use of 'equipment' consisting of just a 'two-penny ha'-penny' forage cap, belt and haversack worn over normal clothing by The Boys' Brigade was not used simply because it was 'cheap'. It suited the prevailing climate of caution with regard to all things military within many churches in the 1880s.[22] Throughout the late nineteenth and early twentieth centuries the major brigades suffered much orchestrated opposition to the alleged 'taint of the Military Spirit' within their work. This was typified by the efforts of a movement called The Knights of the Prince of Peace founded by the Rev. W. J. Spriggs-Smith of Wisbech.[23] But the fact was that the boys loved it. Playing at soldiers was the great attraction. Military men such as General Gordon were regarded as heroes and rôle models.

The boy population of the great towns and cities of Britain in the nineteenth century could not be ignored. In the years between 1841 and 1901 young people averaged over thirty-five per cent of the population. This profile was a constant in an increasingly urbanized population that had, as a proportion of the overall numbers, grown between 1841 and 1901 from 48.3 to 78.00 per cent.[24] The raw material available for new organizations and societies, such as brigades, was seemingly endless. Industrialization also increased the wealth of the country during this period lowering unemployment and creating a lower middle-class and skilled working-class whose children provided a 'new' client group for emerging youth movements. Scotland, which was to be the birthplace of the Boys' Brigade, like many other parts of increasingly prosperous urban Britain, was still divided by class and income. Drummond and Bulloch in their study of the Church in Victorian Scotland[25] describe towns as being divided into four groups; the wealthy, the lower middle-class and the skilled working class '...but there was a fourth group, and this probably the largest of all, who lived in an appalling and secluded poverty, without influence in politics and who, so far as the Christian Church was concerned, were heathen, unless when Roman Catholic.' So, was it just the lower middle-class and skilled working-class which spawned the new brigade organizations? Our evidence suggests that we can also trace brigade origins from initiatives specifically targeted at the vast ranks of those 'heathen' paupers.

Religious revivals, epitomized by visits from evangelists such as Dwight L. Moody and Ira D. Sankey, (between 1873 - 1891) followed each other and these fostered new 'youth' initiatives amongst supporters. Also the 'evils' of the demon drink were addressed by a proliferation of abstinence and temperance movements. Young people were the target of what we would now refer to as 'local initiatives'. Some of these became national and international organizations. Our contention is that many of these, prior to 1883, were indeed prototype or embryonic 'brigades' that served as the models for the Boys' Brigade and its progeny, such as the Church Lads' Brigade, Boys' Life Brigade, Catholic Boys' Brigade and Jewish Lads' Brigade. A selection of these little known and hitherto sparsely covered early 'brigades' is brought together here in this book for the first time. Naturally, no apology is made for focusing upon those elements of organization, content and style that provide a clear and definite link with their later imitators.

CHAPTER TWO

Glasgow Sunday Schools and Institutes

The Boys' Brigade grew directly from the Sunday school movement in Scotland. It is, therefore, important to investigate the Glasgow Sabbath School Union by examining the Annual Reports issued between 1841 and 1890. [26] Also, individual charismatic leaders such as Christian philanthropist Michael Connal played a vital role. Connal, whilst working in the Sunday school movement in the 1840s, quickly realised that a wider approach would need to be taken if young adults ('youths' or 'seniors' as they were described) were to be successfully engaged and encouraged into Christian manhood. Consequently, he became a significant architect of both formal and informal education within his home city. Connal's work covers the change in emphasis in Sunday school work over some forty years from the simple fare of basic education in return for religion, to that of a much broader and more subtle approach to spreading Christianity. In the 1850s others, such as J. Wakefield MacGill, were to follow in Connal's footsteps by adding much more variation to the basic diet of the Sabbath School.

The Glasgow Sabbath School Union

The preamble to the 4th Annual Report of the Glasgow Sabbath School Union, in 1841, stated that it was difficult to say when Sabbath Schools began in Scotland, but certainly, '...*long before their commencement in England.*' There was evidence of their existence in 1782 in both Glasgow and Banchory, and they may have existed even earlier, possibly in 1723 or 1709. Mr Robert Raikes of Gloucester gets the credit for starting the first one in 1783, but he didn't challenge the Scottish claim, and he didn't borrow the idea from Scotland - he'd probably never heard of it. There was most definitely a Sabbath School in the Gallowgate, Glasgow in 1783. The first Glasgow Sabbath School Union was formed on 2nd July 1816 in connection with the Sabbath School Union for Scotland, but it only survived for two years.

In the 1840s, Sunday schools were very popular in Glasgow. There were, in 1841, some 1,325 Teachers and 21, 922 pupils of which nearly half were boys. Much effort was expended to encourage 'attendance and diligence' among the young people. Family visits were common, assisted by the 'local' system, devised by Dr. Chalmers, of dividing the town into districts, with a teacher appointed to each one. The teaching of reading was amongst the main challenges at this time. By 1851, the number of teachers had more than doubled and the number of boys had increased to 16,553 out of a total school population of 36,809. There were 514 schools run by 93 Societies. However, the Annual Report stated that there was a difficulty in retaining 'adults' (those over 15 years). The introduction of more music plus adult classes during the week and evenings was described as, '...*a feeble attempt to meet the growing spiritual destitution of the neglected youth of the city...*' The teaching of reading was still regarded as very important.

The 1860s saw continued growth in the number of Societies. By the end of that decade there were some 55,086 scholars. A wider range of weekly activities was introduced aiming to address the needs of young people through the provision of physical, intellectual and spiritual activities. Annual reports during the 1860s gave even more emphasis to targeting 'lads' by reporting the establishment of a 'Young Men's Institution'. In 1861, it was stated that: '*If the Societies do not thus anticipate the capabilities and tastes consequent on their Scholars emerging from boyhood and girlhood, they need not wonder and complain that their grown-up pupils cannot be retained.*' In September 1870, the 3rd Scottish Sabbath School Convention was held which, among other initiatives, recommended separate infant classes, and 'Young Men's Bible Classes'. It was reported that, out of some 69,992 scholars only 24,768 attended church and consequently services in the 'Forenoon', suitable for youngsters were encouraged. Music Festivals were no longer a novelty, according to the report of 1881. Societies were looking for something else. There was much more stress given to the training of teachers and working with the Foundry Boys' Society. Although levels of reading were much higher, almost certainly due to the introduction of Board Schools, there was an increased disparity between the number of Girls (45,381) and Boys (37,954). The 1882 Report stated that there was, '...*an increased interest on the part of our churches in the work of the Sabbath Schools. We have not, for several years past, been keeping pace, as we ought, with the population.*'

By 1883, the situation of 'Senior Scholars' was regarded by the executive as being acute. In April of that year the 46th Annual Report claimed that whilst past conferences had been called to address current issues -'*Our Senior Boys and Girls, and their Week Evening Occupations. How we can influence them?*' - little interest had been shown. A crusade was needed to '...*stimulate all the Societies in the Union to increased efforts to retain their Senior Scholars.*' Indeed, 1883 - the foundation year for the B.B. - witnessed huge evangelical meetings across the city. There was now a clear recognition that the Sabbath School was the nursery of the Church and the Committee was strongly of the opinion that classes for senior scholars, '...*meeting in rooms separate from the general school*', were essential concomitants of every Sabbath School. The problem was one of accommodation, however, as most meeting places simply didn't have available space. The report contained the type of sentiment and advice which could well have been written by William Smith: *'When young people reach the age of fifteen or thereby, they naturally feel that they are too old to be classed as children, and unless drafted from the general school into a separate class-room for seniors, they generally drop-out of Bible-class tuition and supervision - at what is perhaps the most critical period of their lives.'* Advice offered in the 1884 Report suggested that young people were starting to express themselves when it stated that teachers should be, *'...meeting and checking the rudeness and coarseness which has become so painfully characteristic of our time.'*

In the 1886 Annual Report, both Boys' Brigade and Bands of Hope appeared. In the statistics section it was stated that, *'A number of societies also report having instituted Companies in connection with the Boys' Brigade - a movement which is finding much favour and seems to accomplish much good by training the lads to habits of punctuality, obedience, and order, as well as banding them together with the highest ideal of true Christian manliness and mutual helpfulness in good.'* A year later Boys' Brigade companies were, *'rapidly increasing.'* In 1888, the BB was included in the 'Senior Scholars' section of the report: *'The BB movement, which has proved such a helpful auxiliary to Senior Classes, and Sabbath school work generally, continues to grow and extend; and your Directors desire again very cordially to recommend its adoption by Sabbath School Societies not yet provided with a Boys' Brigade.'* The number of BB Companies within the Union was regularly stated, 1888 - 86 companies, 1889 - 90 companies, 1890 - 97 companies, and 1892 - 94 companies. Nevertheless, commenting on the position of 'Seniors', the 1889 Report bemoaned the fact that 130 out of 317 Societies still had no senior class. The lack of accommodation was given as the main reason.

Connal in 1867

Sir Michael Connal

Connal was involved with two of the first Institutes to be set up in Glasgow. One was established by him in 1848 and another with which he became associated eleven years later. The first, The Spoutmouth Institute, was for young men of the 'artisan' class and the second, The Buchanan Institute, for destitute boys.

The Spoutmouth Bible Institute

Andrew Gillespie's detailed study of Sir Michael Connal, published in 1898, [27] described a man who recognised that there was a future for Christian, informal 'character building' education as an extension of the Sunday school movement. Remarkably, this was some thirty-five years before William Alexander Smith and the Boys' Brigade.

Connal, a Glaswegian, was born on 11th August 1817. He graduated and became a successful businessman in London where he continued to educate himself. Whilst education was very important to Connal, it was his faith which guided his endeavours. Inspired by his 'hero' the charismatic evangelist and 'Disruption' Free Church leader, Dr Thomas Chalmers, Connal saw that there were groups within the growing cities of Scotland which were missing out in both politics and religion. Like Chalmers, Connal not only had a social conscience and a passionate belief, but was also willing to channel a somewhat romantic idealism into practical projects. Certainly some of the fire, magic and vitality which led Chalmers to seek to include all social groups within the church, inspired Connal to do likewise. The Free Church doctrine of 'power to the people'- God helps those who help themselves- dominated his thinking and actions.

On his return to Glasgow, Connal soon became involved with one of the Sabbath School Societies at St. James's Church. He joined as a teacher in Spoutmouth and never left. Schooling in Glasgow in the 1840s was very thin on the ground and the various Societies, like the one at St. James's, were amongst the first to attempt to improve man's circumstances by providing additional education. Visits to the homes of his Sabbath School class of boys and girls opened Connal's eyes to the poverty, ignorance and distress of many families in the area. On the 10th June 1848, full of the scholarly vision and inspiration of Dr. Chalmers, Connal started the 'Spoutmouth Bible Institute', sometimes referred to as 'the Spout' or 'Spout Lads', the aim being to help remedy evils and improve the conditions of life to, '*...quicken their interest in knowledge and desire for improvement in conduct.*' The intention was that the Institute was to be a support group, '*...by friendly life in a humble club.*' Members would be encouraged to help themselves, spare time would be directed and facilities made available. It is, perhaps, interesting to note that 1848 was a year of political unrest throughout Europe. A revolution in France in February had acted as a catalyst for disturbances in many towns and cities including a large demonstra tion by Chartists in Kennington, London, in April. It is possible that there were some elements of 'social control' which led him to choose that significant year to start his Institute.

The first few years of the Institute provided a wide variety of activities for the young artisans of Spoutmouth. Initially it was a small room filled with a variety of newspapers, a reading room for 'the Spoutmouth artisan'. The back room, which was aimed at the men, became a 'howff', that is a place for relaxing and talking. David Logan, a local fruit merchant, supported the venture from the start, although the members were expected to pay 1/- per annum. There were illustrated lectures on Friday evenings, and, by 1851, no fewer than 68 had been delivered. One was given by Professor Henry Drummond on 'How the Earth was built up'. Visits to Art Galleries, Panoramas, and other excursions were organised. The first penny savings bank in Glasgow was started in 1849. There was a library with 300 volumes. In 1851 a Constitution was formulated which spoke of the 'Religious and Intellectual improvement of Young Men.' The Spout was a self-governing group except that the Bible Class teacher had to be chosen by the Church. The emphasis was on young men mastering a new subject and then teaching it - mutual self help. Week-day classes were started covering such subjects as Botany and Chemistry. In 1858, following a chance meeting with Robert Middleton, President of the Sunday School Union, and after taking his advice, Mr J. Wakefield MacGill, the founder and Superintendent of what was to become the Grove Street Home Mission Institute in the Cowcaddens Glasgow arrived eagerly to study the work in 'the Spout'. MacGill was looking for ideas and inspiration to further develop his Ragged School. Writing in 1886 MacGill recalled: *'I was directed to the Spoutmouth, a queer place, off the Gallowgate, now swept away by the City Improvement Trust.'* [28.] On a number of occasions afterwards MacGill played-down the significance of the visit, but there can be no doubt as to the clear and lasting impression it made. In 1866, he wrote of the visit, *'... immediately visited Mr Connal, who invited me to attend the anniversary gathering of his young men. There I heard the full particulars of the organization, and at once set to work on his model.'* [29.] Connal's ideas were spreading. The Grove Street Home Mission became a veritable power-house of Christian evangelism and social work including the inauguration and initial development of the Glasgow Foundry Boys' Religious Society. On 3rd October 1859, a Junior Bible Class for those under sixteen years was formed with members enjoying all the facilities of the Institute. *'The Juniors are a cheerful and faithful band'*, stated Connal,[30] but they were not more than about a dozen. There were some sixteen over the age of six

The Spoutmouth in the 1860s

teen years. About this time Connal became a Volunteer soldier, and one who fancied himself to be a 'sharpshooter'. He would sometimes even attend Sunday school in his uniform! Unlike his Volunteer contemporary, John Hope of Edinburgh, Connal was not anti-Catholic and remained on very good terms with the local people.

Remarkably, a more detailed examination of the activities at the 'Spout' reveals tales of pioneering outdoor education. On Saturday evenings, rambles would take place and there would be songs, jokes and a total disregard of weather conditions as Michael Connal led young men out into the local countryside. He was energetic, enthusiastic and quite eccentric. He ignored bridges and gates, stepping out in a straight line across the fields. Like the inter-war ramblers and cyclists some sixty years later, and with distinct similarities to the Hitler Youth at that time, the purpose was 'character building'. [31] An annual excursion continued the trend, with nobody being 'coddled' and everyone becoming accustomed to joking under any circumstance. On long hikes they would stay in bothy style accommodation, once with nineteen people for just three beds. In 1857, sixty went to Staffa and Iona and at Fingals cave, *'Being given to give vent to their feelings by singing 'Old Hundred', they were dismayed at an irrepressible old highlander who insisted on accompanying them on the bagpipes!'* [32] Other activities were introduced such as elocution and drama classes, Christy Minstrels, a dancing class and an annual 'Social' along with a gymnasium used by 'strong muscular youths'. About 1872, a magazine was started and the Institute became much more outward looking with pupils attending the Buchanan Institute and various other schools. Connal, a member of the school board, encouraged attendance because he viewed the Institute as a help towards the formation of character, which was not available elsewhere. The Spout became very popular and young men came from all over the city causing the Institute to move from one building to another in an attempt to provide adequate accommodation.

Was 'the Spout' the first such organization? The Rev. Arthur Sweatman in his paper 'Youth Clubs and Institutes' read to the Social Science Association in Edinburgh in October 1863 cited the Rev Henry White, of the Chapel Royal, Savoy as the founder of the first Youth's Institute, in Dover in 1857, and another at Charing Cross in 1860. A similar group at Bayswater run by Charles Baker was also mentioned. In addition Sweatman expanded upon the work of 'The Islington Youths' Institute' opened in October 1860.[33] However, the 'Spout' undoubtedly pre-dates them all.

The Buchanan Industrial Institute

James Buchanan who died in 1857 left in his will a sum of £3,000 per annum for ten years to the City of Glasgow to maintain and instruct destitute children in an 'Industrial Institution'. It was also to be an 'Experimental Institution'. If successful, it would gain the remainder of his estate upon the death of his wife.

The Institute was opened in the autumn of 1859 in a large former mansion house at Greenhead, in the vicinity of Glasgow Green. From the start it was controversial. It was seen as a departure from the established ideas of Ragged Schools, Hospital Schools or Reformatories. The City would establish and repair the building, it was to be non-sectarian, boys would live at home, but meals would be provided during the day. Its curriculum included the usual 3R's, but with the addition of navigation, gymnastics, tailoring, shoemaking and carpentry. The governing Board had twelve directors from all interested parties. Michael Connal was on the Board from August 1858 to September 1892 and Chairman of the Governors until his death.

The Buchanan Boys were not Street Arabs as they lived at home. They were not criminals and they were not children of poorly paid unskilled workmen. Pupils, aged between 8 and 13 years, were mainly children of widows with no means of support, or orphans kept out of the poorhouse by a relative or friends, or even illegitimate children with no paternal financial support. They lived within 2-3 miles of the school and were the children of merchants, ministers, doctors, teachers, et al. There was deliberately no uniform or outward badge of identity, seen as a social stigma at the time. A report in 1860 by the Governor and Headmaster, William Leggatt, indicates that the ethos of the school was very important. He insisted that the boys were neat and tidy and took pride in their appearance, '...*we have a drill sergeant who trains all to military exercises for which the new gymnasium on the green presents such admirable and convenient opportunities.*' A penny bank, amongst the first in the city, was started in 1860. According to Springhall [34] we are led to believe that bugle bands and single stick drill were introduced as activities at the Buchanan from the start. Although there is no specific evidence for this, it is a reasonable assumption. Certainly the 1860 report suggests these kinds of military pursuits, and a later publication by the trust [1913] talks about the fine *'esprit de corps'* in the school

The Band - Buchanan Institute 1913

with pictures of the boys' bugle band and single-stick drill squad. Evidence, perhaps, that here was an institution catering for a class of boys higher than the Street Arabs and incorporating a number of elements of informal education into its programme.

Michael Connal was not a 'child rescuer' if rescue is seen simply as physically saving children from a short desperate life surrounded by the squalor of the urban street. However, he certainly admired those who were rescuing children both physically and spiritually. Lord Shaftesbury, Dr. Guthrie, and William Quarrier all appear prominently in his diary between 1871 and 1889, and clearly he held them in high esteem. Connal was much more intent upon the deliberate building of character than filling bellies or teaching literacy. To put it in the words of biographer Andrew Gillespie, *'He recognised in the nature of the Scottish artisan class an intellectual and moral receptiveness which, like the hidden flower roots, lies wanting till the call of spring.'* In the 1880s he attended Boys' Brigade meetings and was suitably impressed as his diary suggests: *'12 April 1887. Dr Donald MacLeod preached to the Boys' Brigade - about 1500 boys present, and about 1000 of an audience - a fine sight. J. Carfrae Alston, the Brigade President, took the lead.'* [35] No doubt he saw the BB as continuing, on a large scale, his pioneering work of bringing the Christian message to working boys, who were, by the late 1880s, less in need of a basic education, but still very much productive ground upon which to sow the seeds of Christian manliness. Connal was a real pioneer of character building Christian youth work. Knighted for his work as chairman of the Glasgow School Board, he died on the 6th July 1893, aged 76.

The Grove Street Home Mission Institute

Inspired by the challenging question posed by Dr Thomas Chalmers - *'How are we to elevate the masses?'*, an enthusiastic seventeen year old medical student and Sunday school teacher, J. Wakefield MacGill, persuaded his Minister at the Barony Free Church, Rev. Dr Norman Macleod, to let him have premises to start evangelistic social work. [36] The date was 1854 and the population of the City of Glasgow, in a few short years had risen from 100,000 to nearly half a million, resulting in enormous social problems. MacGill's 'premises' consisted of a semi-derelict waiting room at Port Dundas, which along with his brother Harry, he set about renovating in order to create a 'Ragged School'. [37] In 1886, recalling his initial thoughts, he described his new 'Parish' as *'...a wilderness of lanes, foundries, mills and slums...'* at the heart of which was his

tiny, '*...mustard seed of a Ragged school.*' MacGill was persistent and alive with the enthusiastic optimism of youth, and he soon got to know the scholars who he had initially rounded-up off the streets, bribed by a warm fire and basic food. He would even visit his boys and girls at night carrying a bulls-eye lantern.[38] By 1856 there were some 130 scholars attending his classes of basic reading and Christian teaching, including classes specially aimed at Factory (Mill) girls. One of the inspirations for MacGill was in the work of the Carruber's Close Mission in Edinburgh which had opened on the 30th May 1858, under the leadership of James Gall, and was from the start planned as an Institute, probably the first in the country. After a visit to see Michael Connal's work at the Spoutmouth in the summer of 1858 he introduced a Young Men's Bible Students' Society which was so successful that there was soon an average attendance of some 250 complete with a Flute Band, Cricket Club, Reading Room and a Temperance Society. MacGill saw the Bible Students' Society as an: '*...important step towards development of the Ragged School into an Institute.*' The name was changed after a few months, to 'Working Men's Religious Society' as it had widened its age remit. However, it was not just the young men who would benefit from the emerging institution. For a few years a number of the older mill girls had been operating reading classes in various locations in the district. In 1858, MacGill visited one such class in what he described as a 'sub

terranean classroom' in the area known as the 'Old Basin' in Port Dundas. The class was run by a girl called Jeanie Dunn who was, during the day, a 'Wincy Weaver' who stood between two looms from 6.00 a.m. until 6.00 p.m. In the evening she gathered together some 16 to 20 mill girls in order to teach them to read and study the Bible. Jeanie was not alone, other mill girls, notably Mary Thomson and Mary Ann Clough, found rooms and opened classes of their own. The three mill - girl teachers so impressed MacGill that he brought them together to form a 'Mill Girls Religious Society'. The new society started in a single house on 1st August 1859 and was run by the young women, a radical decision at the time. [39] Within a short period the number of girls had risen to well over 500. One of the driving forces behind the expansion was Mary Ann Clough the Secretary of the new society. Mary worked most nights of the week in educational classes as well as being a Sabbath school teacher. MacGill describes her as, '...*such a busy, purpose-like, active woman.*' [40] In 1862, it was Mary who, seeing the needs of the foundry boys as being just as great as the mill girls, established, a school for Foundry Boys based initially in a small room in Dobbie's Loan. Eventually 'The Foundry Boys' outgrew the one mission to become a city-wide institution, 'The Foundry Boys' Religious Society' (see Chapter 4).

By the early 1860s J. Wakefield MacGill had personally nurtured a Sabbath School, a Mill Girls' Religious Society, an Abstainer's Society, a Foundry Boys' class and a Mother's Mission. A wide range of different premises was being utilised which included the original room in Port Dundas, a hall in Corn Street, the Olympic Singing Saloon and the Colosseum Singing Saloon. Some of the facilities were really quite unsuitable for the work. Clearly there was a need for a single building that could accommodate all the varied classes and initiatives and so a committee was formed to erect a 'Home Mission Institute'. Funds were not slow in appearing and on 28th May 1866 the new premises, able to hold nearly 3000 people were opened. The Mission which had cost £10,000 comprised four halls and seventeen classrooms for the use of some 300 volunteer workers. Carved into the stone on the front of the building was the motto: '*Bear ye one another's burdens*' from Galatians 6 v. 2. This was the great self-improvement by self-help ethos upon which the whole establishment had been founded. Work in the Mission was divided into 'departments', which at the opening in 1866 were listed as:

1. Sabbath School (1854)
2. Working Men's Religious Society (1858)
3. Mill Girls' Religious Society (1859)

4. Mother's Mission (1861)
5. Foundry Boys' Religious Society (1865)
6. Abstainer's Society [General] (1860)
7. Evangelistic Work [General] (1860)
(Evangelistic Work, 1868)

The Grove Street Home Mission Institute, in Woodside, a non-sectarian institution founded to reach and elevate the whole family was up and running, and J. Wakefield MacGill it's first 'General Superintendent'.

Back in 1860 the first 'gypsy trip' to Arran had been organised during the Glasgow Fair Holiday in Whit week. The whole idea was to remove as many working men as possible from the temptations of drink in what was described as 'Satan's Season'.[41] On that first occasion 120 men, women, children and babies shared two large tents. However, Scottish weather conditions soon saw-off the larger of the two tents and the whole party, soaked to the skin, was not settled until after midnight on the first day, with the women and children on the floor of the parish schoolroom. Over the years the annual trip grew in popularity, at one stage involving more than 600. After the first few years MacGill extended his excursions to involve special trips for the Mill Girls and the Foundry Boys. As he stated in 1886: *'Then we organised the foundry boys...placing over them a band of respectable men. We selected those who had been in the volunteer force, so that they might control the boys and keep them under discipline.'* [42]

The 18th Annual Report [43] provided an insight to the detailed working of the Institute. The Children's 'Department' as it became known, mainly concerned itself with Sunday school and religious services. There were some 400 children and 21 teachers attending the 9.30 a.m. classes. In the afternoon there was a Children's Service at 2.00 p.m. having between 700 and 1000 children in attendance. Even amongst children under the age of 13 years there was, seemingly, a problem with the behaviour of some. There was a charge of 1d levied for a hymnbook and an attendance stamp was put on it to, *'...keep out those lads who often come to create disturbance.'* [44] When the children were older they moved up to the Mill-Girls or Boys' Religious Society. Initially there had been an emphasis upon learning the '3 R's' but, by 1877, with the introduction of the School Board, the whole emphasis of the work with older boys and girls had started to change to take on a format not at all dissimilar to that of the Boys' Brigade, still some six years away.

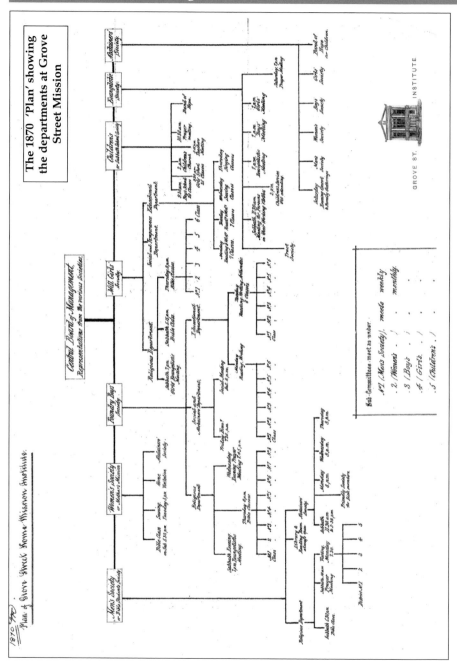

The 1870 'Plan' showing the departments at Grove Street Mission

Looking at the programme for the boys, in comparison to the later Boys' Brigade, there is a great similarity, even to extent of uniform and drill in the Foundry Boys' Department. The boys met for their bible class night on Tuesdays for ten months of the year, and in 1877 it was noted that there was a huge demand with 13 teachers and 190 lads. Significantly, the 1877 Report observed that, *'It is a joy to see the mellowing of character…'*. There was a Christian Union meeting on Saturday evenings and an evangelistic Service on Sunday evenings when 100 boys would hold the meeting themselves. For three nights a week there was a 'Home Room' available with games, books and a good fire. Teachers were present and were, it was said, able to gain insight into the character of a boy and break down any reserve. A Library, with a membership cost of one shilling, made books available on a weekly basis. In 1877, ninety of the boys went to Kilchattan Bay for five days where they had already been three times before. A tent was used for a dining hall and the barn of Largizean Farm for sleeping. Activities included boating, bathing, scrambling and games. Perhaps, needless to say for an Institute built upon abstinence and temperance, the 'Band of Hope' was a great success. Technically speaking, it was a part of the work of the Scottish branch of the 'Order of the Sons of Temperance' started in the USA, but which came under the unifying banner of the Scottish Band of Hope Union in 1871 (see Chapter 7).

In 1886, MacGill listed the activities in operation at the Institute in the early years:

Two Ragged Schools
A large Service for Children, superintended by 150 monitors
A Band of Hope
(with Cadets of Temperance, Daughters of Temperance, Buds of promise.)
Mill-girls' Bible Classes
Sewing Classes
Reading and Writing Classes
Cooking Classes
Bible Classes for Foundry Boys
Education Classes
Singing Classes
Drill etc
Young Men's Bible Class
Gymnasium
Mutual Improvement Society
Mother's Bible Classes
Dorcas Meetings
Temperance Meetings for Women
Working Men's Bible Class
Clubroom
Friendly Societies

Evangelistic Services
Temperance Meetings for Men
Social Meetings
Musical Meetings [45]

MacGill summed up the work thus:

'Such then was our Ragged School, and such were the ways through which God led it, and by which it was developed into a powerful, united, permanent, and most effective agent for rescuing the lost, preventing female degradation, educating the ignorant, training the young, and leavening the substratum of our social life with those glorious Gospel truths, the power of which makes good fathers, holy mothers, virtuous girls, industrious lads, sincere Christians, and good citizens.' [46]

The Grove Street Institute in 1895 - with the new wing

MacGill moved to take up an appointment as Secretary of the Manchester City Mission in 1884, where he remained until 1901, when at the earnest request of the members of Grove St., he returned. He died on 6th March 1902.[(K)] In 1895, a new wing at Grove St. was opened next to the original mission, on the corner of Balnain Street which was used as a homeless people's shelter. It also featured a gymnasium, library and a doctor's consulting room. The Grove Street Institute building continued to be used for its original purpose for more than a century before being demolished in the 1970s.

CHAPTER THREE

Ragged/Industrial Schools

Any study of the roots of the Boys' Brigade would be quite incomplete without more than a passing reference to the so-called 'Ragged' Schools. The authors doubt that there would have been any Boys' Brigade had it not been for these quite worthy institutions. In keeping with the overall purpose and central theme of this volume, an emphasis will be placed upon the history and development of the Scottish branches of these, inasmuch as they have played their part in the origination of the BB. Histories of the Ragged Schools already exist and it is not the intention to provide another.

The idea of Ragged Schools, that is schooling for the poor, has a long pedigree. C. J. Montague in his exhaustive history of the Ragged School Movement, 'Sixty Years in Waifdom' [47] quotes Lord Shaftesbury in the 1846 Quarterly Review, *'We are not able to say when exactly the first beginning was made, nor to apportion the merit of the earliest efforts.'* Certainly, the ragged schools 'exclusively for children raggedly clothed' run by the London City Mission were amongst the first to be officially recognised.[48] Prior to the existence of the L.C.M., formed in 1835, ragged schools existed as part of the Sunday school movement and clearly the schools of the 1840s were direct successors.

The real ethos of the Ragged School movement seems to be epitomised by one man, John Pounds (1766-1839) cobbler and part-time schoolmaster of St. Mary Street, Portsmouth. Pounds worked in the 1820s and '30s. Taking pity on the outcast children who ran wild on the streets, he took them in and trained them in shoemaking skills as well as feeding and educating them. Pounds also loaned them clothing for Sunday school and encouraged them, when practicable, to work in the fresh air. This holistic approach puts him at the forefront of Ragged School pioneers. It was clear to the early philanthropists that the children needed feeding first of all, and this became the initial attraction. It was also regarded as essential that a large percentage of the education would need to be of a practical nature if the young street Arabs were to rise out of poverty.

By 1851 there were about 30 towns and cities in the UK using the Ragged School System. Most of these schools were staffed by volunteers and very lowly paid workers. Some national personalities, such as General Gordon who worked in Gravesend between 1865 and 1871, became   directly involved in teaching, were very influential and able to publicize the cause in the highest circles. Writers and dynamic 'muscular Christian' personalities like John MacGregor were also involved with the Ragged School Union from its earliest

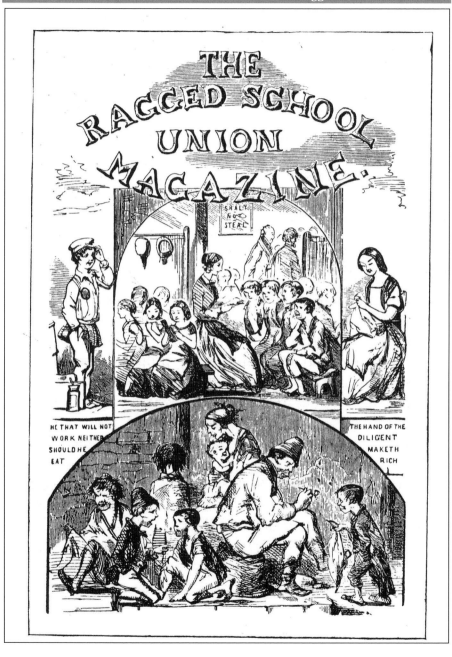

days in the mid -1840s. MacGregor, was seen, and indeed saw himself, as a man of action as well as of words, in his approach to ragged schools. MacGregor expounded the virtues of ragged schools offering a distinctly practical curriculum. In his book 'Ragged Schools; their Rise, Progress, and Results' (1855), MacGregor stated:

'Intellectual teaching is feeble in the work of reformation. The hand and eye must be taught to work as well as the head stored with book-learning, and a school which has no Industrial Class leaves an essential part of the engine of improvement unemployed.'

His chapter on 'Shoe-black Brigades' explained in some detail how in furtherance of his practical ideals, he extended the branches of the Ragged School Tree to include boys who had left the schools and how a similar 'adjunct' to the three Ragged/Industrial Schools of Edinburgh was started by David Harris. [49] It was usual for the founders of Ragged Schools to be Christian gentlemen who were guided by both compassion and evangelistic zeal. If children could read, then they could read the Bible and be taught about Christianity. In the last chapter the work of one of these pioneers in Glasgow, J. Wakefield MacGill, the founder of the Grove Street Home Mission Institute was described in detail. MacGill started with a simple, one-roomed Ragged school and expanded his operations to meet the massive need which surrounded it in the filthy hellish streets of

The scene inside a Ragged School

1850s Cowcaddens. Initially a Sabbath school for children, the Grove Street operation was, within a few years, catering for the whole family.

Perhaps one of the most well-known, or 'infamous' early Ragged schools was the Field Lane school in Saffron Hill, London, well-known to John MacGregor, and the original supplier of his Shoe-black Brigade boys. Established as a Sabbath and Ragged school in 1841, it was in an area of great poverty - the area in which author Charles Dickens set his 'Fagin's den'. Dickens visited the school and as a result of what he found there, wrote an article which appeared in The Daily News on 13th March 1852. Typically, Dickens was able to picture the scene in words:

'The close, low chamber at the back, in which the boys were crowded, was so foul and stifling as to be, at first, almost insupportable. But its moral aspect was so far worse than its physical, that it was soon forgotten. Huddled together on a bench about the room, and shown out by some flaring candles stuck against the walls, were a crowd of boys, varying from mere infants to young men; sellers of fruit, herbs, Lucifer-matches, flints; sleepers under the dry arches of bridges; young thieves and beggars - with nothing natural to youth about them: with nothing frank, ingenuous, or pleasant in their faces; low-browed, vicious, cunning, wicked; abandoned of all help but this; speeding downward to destruction; and UNUTTERABLY IGNORANT.' [50]

BARONESS BURDETT-COUTTS.

Boys on the Training Ship 'Chichester'

Dickens was one of the high-profile philanthropists sponsored for many years by the 'Lady Unknown', [51] - the bank heiress Angela Burdett Coutts. Poor and neglected children were always a particular concern for Burdett-Coutts. Dickens, who described her as *'The noblest spirit we can ever know'*, [52] encouraged her to subsidize the Ragged School Union, started in 1844, and took her to see for herself the squalid poverty of child waifs in London. She actively helped the shoe-black brigades to provide employment, and in 1874 made a first contribution of £5000 for a scheme to train poor boys to be sailors by buying the training ship 'Chichester'. Aware that starving children could not learn or work properly, she became president of the Destitute Children's Dinner Society, founded in 1866 and was an early patron of the London Society for the Prevention of Cruelty to Children, founded in 1883.

The Edinburgh Original Ragged School

Dr. Guthrie began his Edinburgh ragged school work in 1847 initially using methods based on those used by Sheriff Watson of Aberdeen in 1841, which in turn was similar to that of John Pounds. As Guthrie's 'pleas for ragged schools' were published they were taken-up nationally by those who could see that there was an important 'social service' element in what is meant by a ragged school.

Guthrie was particularly concerned about the number of Juveniles who were sent to prison. In his book *'Seed time and Harvest'* Guthrie detailed just how much these youngsters were taking from the community and the cost of bringing them to justice. He was able to provide figures for Edinburgh where his school opened in the summer of 1847. The percentage of children under 14 years of age in prison fell from 5.6 to 0.9 in 1851. Guthrie's pleas were convincing:

'...It seems like lowering a noble cause to introduce the consideration of money to plead for it on the score of economy. It is a great stoop to come down from the lofty heights of Religion, Pity, Humanity, Justice, and Mercy, to pounds shillings and pence. Yet I can demonstrate that ours, the kindest and holiest, is also the cheapest policy. It has been calculated, as I have already stated, that every child left to grow up into a criminal costs the country, on average, not less than three hundred pounds.'

Reports are available which provide an insight into the workings of the school. [53] In the first Report the priority and importance of feeding the boys was emphasised. Later reports detailed the industrial training given and stated that they could not be sent to the colonies without a trade. In 1861, school clothing for these 5 - 14 year olds, was described as a 'plain fustian suit' which went into

The Ragged School Tree - rooted in the Bible, with its many branches
including the Shoe-black Brigade.

a canvas bag at the end of the day and hung on a numbered peg in the corridor. There was a band: '...*a number of the boys are learning music and have been formed into a band; and the said band, playing spirit-stirring airs, precedes the school in its perambulations of the principal thoroughfares of Edinburgh.*' * Writing in 1874 Mr James Wallace (advocate) stated that he had experience of Ragged School boys: '*For the last three or four years I have taught in the Sunday evening school...I do not pretend to say that the boys are all paragons and that we have no difficulty with them on Sunday evenings, but certainly we should have much greater difficulty if it were not for the admirable way in which they were grounded during the week. ...I have noticed...the spirit which the boys and girls exhibit towards the school; there is a great deal of esprit de corps about them - that grand spirit which has been so useful in our army and navy and other public services. The boys and girls are proud to belong to the Ragged School...*'. He went on to say that the problem was in the post-14 year group.

It has long been held as established fact that the Boys' Brigade, in seeking to foster 'esprit de corps', was copying the best Public Schools of the day. Here, nine years before the BB, it seems to be taken for granted that this should exist, even in a Ragged School, and that there was a great need for it in the post fourteen age group. There were, in 1878, some 240 boys and 90 girls all in dormitories in the school. By 1880 the band had improved so much as to become a full brass band and the boys themselves went out and collected the very healthy sum of £45.00 in 14 days to buy new instruments. In 1883, the year the Boys' Brigade's birth, six juvenile bagpipers were introduced to the band. Over the next few years the Brass and Pipe bands improved and were able not only to cover costs, but also to earn cash for the emigration fund and, in addition, provide a healthy surplus for the band's use.

The United Industrial School of Edinburgh

An alternative to the Guthrie Ragged School, the 'United Industrial School of Edinburgh' was set up in 1847. This was a rather bold experiment in that it taught Catholic and Protestant together for all subjects other than Religious Instruction. [54] It was run within the Whig-Liberal tradition of tolerance by those who opposed sectarianism. The aims, naturally, were similar to the Guthrie School: the rescue of street Arabs and to make them moral and industrious members of the working class. The title 'Ragged' was particularly avoided as it was seen as being a humiliating way to brand its children. The age-range was 6 - 14 years, and in 1848 there were 100 children attending, two thirds of them boys. Producing some sort of 'order' in the school was always a great problem. Although there was no uniform as such, right from the start the school adopted a number of 'militaristic' methods to create discipline. *'The boys go through a semi-military exercise of marching, forming into file, etc., with much smartness and precision … Much of the promptness which they exhibit is the effect of the military sort of training to which they are daily subjected by the Inspector* (sic)' [meant 'Superintendent'].[55] During the average day between 9 - 10 a.m., The Superintendent, *'…puts them through a sort of semi-military drill which has been found very serviceable in teaching them habits of obedience, order, celerity, and combined action. It embraces calishetic exercise, is healthy and cheerful, and much in favour with the children.'* [56] Some thirty two years later some of these words, and all of

Vagrant children - 'Street Arabs'

the sentiment would appear in the Boys' Brigade object. Drill was a regular feature and is reported right through until the 1890s.[57] Coincidentally, whilst the boys were drilling, the girls cleaned the house!

In the decade following 1851 the Edinburgh Industrial School had to incorporate a number of changes.[58] In 1854, as the result of an Act of Parliament, vagrant children were being sent by Magistrates, making it partly a 'Reformatory School'. William Maxwell the Superintendent died in 1857 and was replaced by Headmaster Mr. Charles Ferguson. The school was not to give up on drill however, because, in 1858, a Drill Sergeant, Mr. Bremner, was appointed as a full-time post. The initial concept of children living at home, in an attempt to reform the parents, was thrown out in 1859 because the negative influence of those parents was destroying the good work being done. In any case, children sent by the courts required constant supervision. Dormitories were initiated in 1860. Numbers in 1863 were reported as being the highest ever and the balance between criminals and non-criminals was changing in favour of the former. In the 1871 Report there was the first mention of a band: '...selected number of boys who perform very creditably as a Flute Band.' Presumably the band boys wore a uniform because the HMI Report of 1872 stated that, during regular activities, 'Many of the boys were ragged and careless as to their dress.' A Band Master was appointed in 1873 at £25.00 a year which was £10 more than the Music Teacher. The band's efficiency was praised in the 1875 Report, but in the same year it was stated that boys had never been properly clothed by the school. One reason given was that uniform amounted to 'disciplinarian repression'. It should be noted that this view existed when the BB was founded and even continues today. By 1875 there was a much wider range of activities which would today be described as 'recreation'. Cricket, football, swimming, gymnastics and trips to Queen's Park and Portobello were all reported. A trip to the country, to Musselburgh, for three weeks in the summer of 1881 indicates a growing trend towards giving the boys an outdoor experience. A swimming bath was opened at the school in 1882 which is quite astonishing considering that George Watson's College, one of Edinburgh's most famous private schools, didn't get its pool until fifty years later! [59] A full brass band was started in 1889 following a suggestion that boys well trained in a brass band could find good employment in army or navy bands.

In 1904, the statistics for the remaining 151 schools in membership of the Ragged School Union included 22 Boys' Brigade Companies with a total of 837 lads. [60]

*Footnote on Marching Bands

Bands, as can be determined from the information above, featured strongly in the extra-curricular activities of the Ragged & Industrial Schools. Marching and uniforms were accepted as a method of steering young people, particularly boys, into being moral and responsible members of society. In fact, marching, music lessons and band practice were often part of the timetabled day. All types of band became a feature of many of the early Boys' Brigade companies and for many people, even in the twenty-first century, bands and the Boys' Brigade are synonymous.

Opinion as to the appropriate nature of the marching band for young people has always been divided, as has the provision of anything for those who only have little.[61] The Scotsman printed a letter concerning the band of the Original Edinburgh Ragged School which clearly indicates that not everyone favoured a band for paupers:

OUR RAGGED SCHOOL ARISTOCRACY

Edinburgh, August 6, 1861

'SIR, - It has happened to me in the course of my walks to see and also hear a fine band of young persons parading the city with that pomp and air of conscious superiority which martial music inspires and orderly marching gives expression to. I ask who they are, and am told they are the pupils of a ragged school. Ragged school! Bless you, I defy the most aristocratic academy in the country to produce a finer turn-out. Everything - toggery, Instruments, the great drum, and the important looking fellow who bears and thumps it - the music itself - the whole, in short, in such perfect style, as if expense were no consideration when weighed against good taste. There is a crowd always to look at the affair, and many a hard-worked message boy and anxious printer's devil, who has to labour long hours and fall to sleep on hall-chairs waiting for proofs, gives a wistful look at the fortunate members of that gay procession. Nay, I am not sure but that I could sometimes detect in the eye of the hard-working artisan, going home to his frugal dinner and his responsibilities, a look expressing how gratified he would be to see his own grimy urchins in that distinguished flock. I know, sir, that when I was a boy, it would have been the ambition of my life to belong to that band. True, I must have qualified for it. The civil service and every good thing requires a qualification either in the obtainer or in some other person. If my parents had not by improvidence or profligacy sent me to the streets, I must have gone to the streets of my own device and become a mendicant or a pickpocket. Boys are but men, as some one says. I am not prepared to say how far I should have been able to resist the temptation.

Doubtless the band is a very nice thing to those who are in it. It would be possible to find many other ways, too of smoothing and elevating their path in life. They might be taught dancing, fencing, riding, callisthenics, deportment, composition, the art of conversation, and all gentlemanly accomplishments. They might be trained in languages and sciences, so as to be fitted for diplomacy, the learned professions, or the civil service. All this would be elevating their position. Why not give it them? My own answer is, that as there are two sides to every question, there are in everything that is of a repressive or reformatory character emphatically two sides - the inside and the out-side. Weighing duly the interests of both, I would consider that I was doing my best to injure the community if I gave a penny of my money to support that band. - I am, &c. ARISTIPPUS

P.S. - I see that in his last report, Her Majesty's Inspector of Reformatories regrets "the uniform clothing which the children wear in the school and the band which has been formed among them." "I fear," he says, "this may act unfavourably upon the parents, and make it rather a mark of distinction than inferiority to attend the school." Surely such a remark, coming from such an authority, claims the grave consideration of the managers of the school, if not of the public at large.'

The Brompton Boys' Institute Band c.1910

CHAPTER FOUR

The Glasgow Foundry Boys' Religious Society

It was a pleasant day in Glasgow Fair Week. The venue was the seat of the Duke of Argyll at Inveraray and the distinctive trill of a fife band could be heard in the distance. As the sound grew nearer people emerged from the background. It was clearly a parade, a parade of boys, all marching smartly in time to the beating drum. A large flag was proudly borne behind the band. The military bearing, drill and appearance of the boys seemed to be enhanced by the uniforms. The older boys were attired in tunics with varying numbers of stripes denoting their rank - one, two or three - adorned with a row of buttons. Each had a leather waist - belt and on their heads they were wearing army style 'pill-box' forage caps. Most of the boy-contingent appeared resplendent in best Sunday clothing over which was worn 'equipment' consisting of a belt, pill-box cap and over the right shoulder of each boy, a distinctive white canvas haversack strap. An adult leader, the 'Captain', barked out the command 'Parade... Halt'. The band ceased playing and the whole column halted smartly as one. The adult then led the boys in a few moments of prayer before they fell-out to eagerly consume rations, which appeared magically, from their former place of concealment in the pockets of the haversacks. Clearly, this was a typical Boys'

From a faded photograph - Fair Week Trip to Inveraray 1866

Brigade 'March Out' of the 1880s or 1890s, or even early 20th century. However, such an assumption would be mistaken. For this was 1869 (actually it might have been three years earlier minus the band) and the Boys' Brigade had not yet been 'invented'.

The boys marching to Inveraray in 1869 were members of the Glasgow Foundry Boys' Religious Society (GFBRS) an organisation which today still exists with a headquarters located at 15, Tharis St. Glasgow G21. (L) The GFBRS has been called the first of two initiatives in the renewal of the Sunday School movement. The first came from the Army and the second from The Boys' Brigade.[62] However, this analysis denies the other organisations any input and perhaps over-emphasises the role played by the army - the 'Volunteers' - in this revival.

In 1860, Mary Ann Clough a mill worker from Cowcaddens then on Glasgow's northern outskirts, was the Secretary of the Mill Girls' Religious Society and a Sabbath School teacher at the mission. The area was an unpleasant mixture of foundries, mills and slum houses. Mary Ann had come into contact with a determined evangelical pioneer called J. Wakefield MacGill who had helped her to establish the Mill Girls' Religious Society in the previous year. She was, however, very concerned about the hundreds of lads who worked in the foundries. MacGill, writing in 1886 summed up the situation:

'But outside there was a great unattached constituency of wild, uncared-for boys ... In connection with the foundries there is a vast population of boys - wild, thoughtless lads- who literally care neither for God nor man; whose hands are ready for mischief, and whose mouths are an open sepulchre...Fourteen years of practical work has forced upon us the belief that the Sunday School is utterly unable to combat the evil influences operating upon our juvenile population...who spend the greater part of their early days in "Satan's training ground" [The Streets]...at that most important and critical time of their lives when they are too great, in their own eyes, to attend a Sunday school, and too young to be identified with adult organisations.' [63]

MacGill had hit upon the same need identified again by William Smith some twenty three years later. Mary Ann Clough approached MacGill on numerous occasions saying to him, *'Mr MacGill, is nothing to be done for the foundry boys?'* The foundry boys were a rough lot -*'rough boys in an ugly world'*. [64] In 1866, the 'Self Help' magazine described the foundry boys: *'...between ten and twelve they enter the foundries, which are the academies of sin and blasphemy, where the cur*

rent is all downwards, and where the juvenile rivalry is to outvie the roughest and most licentious of their men-models in words and deeds of profanity and impurity.' [65] Some months went by and no man had volunteered to take-up the cause of the foundry boys and so, on the suggestion of MacGill, Mary Ann Clough decided to do something herself. She obtained the use of a room below the factory where she worked and opened it on Sunday afternoons for a *"Little meeting of Working Boys"*. Some 35 lads attended and Mary Ann soon got to know them and their families. Influential people, such as Dr. Guthrie, quickly began to respect Mary Ann for her work, marvelling at the success she had achieved, and those who knew her were able to explain that the secret of Mary Ann's power was - *'she was a woman!'* Her charges were often referred to as 'Mary Ann's Boys'. In 1862, Mary Ann emigrated to New Zealand and her direct influence in Glasgow ended. Her work, however, was continued in the foundries by James Hunter, who like William Smith was in the business of buying and selling shawls and wraps. His work was reported in the 'Sunday at Home' Magazine in 1888: *'...the late Mr James Hunter, who for months held Sabbath classes, weekday evening classes, penny bank and flute band, in the hall of a foundry granted by foundry masters, where night after night he met the boys employed in the works.'* [66] Unfortunately, James Hunter's single-handed initiative, *'...died down to feebleness'.* [67]

On 21st November 1865, James Hunter along with three friends, William P. Hunter, Alexander Mackieth and William Martin met to revive Mary Ann Clough's initiative and to draw-up a plan to widen and extend the Foundry Boy work she had started. Their object for the society being, *'...the religious, educational and social elevation of the poor neglected boys employed in the foundries and workshops of the city.'* No doubt the four men were proposing to use the forthcoming purpose-built Grove Street Mission building. An account of the first meetings of the re-formed society, which was fortunately recorded, makes absorbing reading however; because the new building was not yet open.

'Our first Sunday meeting with the boys was held in a dingy, deserted singing saloon, in the Cowcaddens, known as the Olympic Hall, which, though very unsuitable, was the best accommodation we could obtain at the time. In the general appearance of the place there was everything to dispel any serious feelings, but the boys seemed in no need of any incitement to noise and misbehaviour. We need not speak of their conduct outside the hall, as that was rather beyond our control; but what it was may be gathered from the fact that a clergyman, who had long successfully conducted a mission in close proximity to our place of meeting, wrote us, threatening to complain to the police of our

A Foundry Boy of the 1860s

nightly assembling such a disorderly rabble... And then, when the doors were opened, in a style that would have petrified most people, and which even astonished those long used to deal with such rough boys, about 100 of them assembled, more as if some comic piece were to be acted which would be much improved by a little by-play on their part. The clatter of clogs, the promiscuous shouts of "Haw Jock" - "Wull" - "Come 'ere, Tam", - the diving under the gallery seats into the vacancy below, and the successful practical jokes thereby possible, made a most appalling beginning. The chairman on the stage, striving to reduce the chaos to order, was more like a captain shouting orders from the gangway in a hurricane; but, eventually, order was obtained, though of a most brittle kind at first. A strange cough, any extra noise from some latecomer, a dog barking outside and such unforeseen circumstances, set our friends up in a moment, either to join in the disturbance, or, with mock desire for order, roaring "pit him oot, pit him oot", "Hear him noo"'. [68]

The religious meeting was only one aspect or 'Department' of early GFBRS work. In fact, the whole tenet of the GFBRS was that Sabbath schools didn't work by themselves. The first Annual Report states clearly:

'...something in addition to the Sabbath School is required ... If we desire to keep or raise these boys, we must meet them on their own ground, presenting some

thing adapted to their embryo manhood ...Christianity...must wear an attractive drapery of social recreation and amusement and prove that religion and education are blessed and happy powers which, far from rendering life sombre and joyless, gives a fresh zest and keener appetite for all that is ennobling and good.' William Smith could quite easily have written these words, some eighteen years later.

The four departments of the GFBRS were based on a similar system used at the Grove Street Home Mission Institute as described in chapter two. Since most of the boys were regarded as 'ignorant', classes in reading, writing and arithmetic were soon established and extended as an 'Education Department'. By January 1866 so successful had the organisation become that it was desperately seeking a move to larger rooms.[69] Those requirements for expansion would soon be amply met with the opening of the new Grove Street Home Mission Institute building, Woodside, in May of the same year. The Self Help magazine for working people published that year detailed the requirements for working with the foundry boys: *'No work of this kind need be attempted without proper rooms, specially got up for the purpose, a large number of foundry boys in a hall would certainly prove a failure; but if a body of earnest working men, and each eight or ten lads in a little room of his own, he*

The first Flute Sergeant in the GFBRS - 1868

would soon win them by affection, and mould them at his will.' (M) The hope was expressed that in the new building the work could be re-started. 70

In fact, the work had already been re-started, astonishingly in that very same large unsuitable singing saloon hall. However, upon eventually moving into the new premises on 3rd June 1866 a new regime was immediately insti-gated by the four leaders. A formal admission procedure was introduced with parents being visited. The rules were established that every boy must attend a religious meeting on the Sabbath and pay a subscription of 2d weekly. To make maximum use of time and space, the education programme was quite regi-mented, involving the rotational use of rooms, with boys calling off numbers and marching in and out of the classrooms. The boys were classified, *'...accord-ing to deficiency...and then classified by size...grown lads will not stand beside little boys.'* Meetings started at 7.30 p.m. every Monday, Tuesday and Wednesday. Boys stopped work at 6 p.m., but unwashed and hungry they came to the hall, shouted out their society numbers at the roll-keepers table and were then issued with pens and copy books. The older boys occupied the side rooms, but everyone changed rooms halfway through and all were finally marched out in orderly ranks at 9 p.m..71

Drill was considered to be an essential part of a 'Social Reform' depart-ment, which included the Total Abstinence Society, entertainments and excur-sions, and a Saturday Evening Club. Drill, the founders explained:

'... is a most important and elevating feature of our scheme. The good effect of drill in implanting a habit of ready and unquestioning obedience can be easily understood by all, while those who have had experience in "the ranks" know how valuable it is in giv-ing order and ease of management to what would otherwise be a disorderly mob. This part of the work is under the command of a few volunteer friends, assisted by a drill instructor, and is much liked by the boys.' 72

Initially the Waterloo Street Drill Hall, home of the 1st Lanarkshire Artillery Volunteer Regiment, was used even though it was a mile from the Sunday meeting place and two miles from the schoolroom. *'The boys eagerly attended, and became remarkably proficient in the simpler movements.'* Average attendance at drill was by 1869 some 80 boys and the uniform had become a little more elaborate. It was described thus:

'A cheap uniform, consisting of tunic, cap and belt, is provided for the boys by the

Society and it remains in the Society's possession, the boys paying for and keeping the uniform trousers, which average from 5s to 7s a pair.'

According to Springhall, [73] by the early 1870s the use of uniform and drill in the GFBRS seems to have died out in some branches, although this may have not have been the case universally. The involvement of girls in the organisation from 1870 was probably a major reason for the decline in 'masculine' activities such as drill, although there was still at least one drill class of 20 boys operating in 1880 at the Grove Street premises, [74] and an active Flute Band with 47 members and regular practices. [75]

The first Annual Report of the society mentioned that as part of the 'Social Reform' activities the boys were given free admission to the Working Men's Industrial Exhibition which took place from 1865 - 1866 and 150 of them went, *'… in companies on three different nights under the command of their captains… .'* Clearly the military terminology which would eventually be taken up by The Boys' Brigade was in use from the start of the GFBRS. [76]

In the summer months, upward of 150 boys would turn out for an afternoon and march through the suburbs. Parks were used for drill and games of football and cricket. Excursions were organised, the main one being a week long annual camp held at Inveraray during the Glasgow Fair Week. The idea of the Fair-Week trip was to remove the boys from all the drunkenness and lewd behaviour that so characterised that holiday period. *'Anxious consideration'* had been given as to how the society could, *'…take them away for the whole week from scenes of temptation.'* The cost to the boys was 5s and on the Friday morning, *'…90 boys and a committee of gentlemen left Glasgow…and spent a happy and memorable week amidst the beauties of Inveraray and Lochfyne, returning home bronzed and beaming with health to the city, not a single casualty or a temporary sickness being occurred to mar the week's enjoyment.'* Dr Guthrie, even though aged 63 and in less than perfect health, was present for the whole week and wrote to the 'Sunday Magazine' in February 1867: *'Attired in a uniform and with the smart air of those that had gone through drill, the boys presented a remarkably neat appearance; while their young faces, usually begrimed with the dust and smoke of foundries, were bright as a May morning, and beamed with happiness'.* [77]

The first Fair-Week trip to Inveraray, was also reported in the Glasgow Herald, where it stated that each boy was enabled to appear, *'…in military dress, with a haversack containing the day's provisions, and with a blanket etc rolled in a towel and carrying a knapsack. Notwithstanding the peaceful flag floating over-head, they had a very military appearance, and throughout it was remarked how much the drill added to the orderliness and good management of the trip. On arrival at Lochgoilhead, an easy march through the wild scenery of "Hell's Glen" brought the lit-tle army to St. Catherine's, where the 'Fairy' awaited them and speedily steamed across Loch Fyne to Inveraray.'* [78] The boys slept in church halls and parish schools and were welcomed by the locals who called them 'Glesc's Keelies'. [79] The 1868 Fair-Week trip included two local flute bands and included boys from Cowcaddens, Gorbals, Anderston and Bridgeton. These vigorous outdoor activities were a very important and attractive feature of the Society, which, by 1870, had 36 separate groups and 12,000 members located in various parts of Scotland. By this time it should be noted that girls were being allowed to join and the Fair-Week excursion in 1870 took 70 girls to Inveraray and 130 boys to Strachur.

The fourth department was the 'Provident' where habits of saving were encouraged and a Savings Bank opened by the Society. Every boy was issued

Above: A competition-medal issued by the GFBRS. Left & Below: Activities included camping and gymastics.

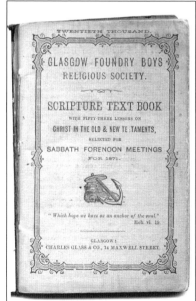

Gymnastic Drill.

Left: The GFBRS Scripture Text Book for 1871 with its Anchor emblem. From 1872 the anchor pictured right became used more frequently on publications.

with a Member's Pass Book which was also the Bank Book. There were a number of 'Cheap Schemes' available to them for the purchase of clothes and boots at 'wholesale rates'. Bibles were supplied by the National Bible Society of Scotland.

The Earl of Shaftesbury visited Glasgow in 1871 and John Burns informed him and the public that the GFBRS...

'...has organised a system of Sabbath Religious meetings, week-day education classes, drill exercises, savings banks, summer excursions, winter evening exhibitions, soirees, musical, social and temperance meetings and singing classes'.[80]

The 15th Annual Report of the GFBRS published in 1881 identified some 66 *'Co-operating Churches and Associations'* within the Glasgow area, the largest group being from the Free Churches, and the object had become, *'...the Religious, Educational, and Social Elevation of Boys and Girls.'* [81] Interestingly, it listed the Adelaide Place Baptist Church which would, just a few years later, close down the newly established '3rd Glasgow Boys' Brigade' because it was too militaristic. Generally, the sentiment was very positive, and when Smith founded his Boys' Brigade in 1883 the leaders of the GFBRS were amongst the first to welcome the initiative.[82] It was J. B. Couper, a leader of the GFBRS in the Anderston area who, as well as being a member of the 1st Lanark Rifle Volunteers like Smith, instigated the formation of the second company in January 1885. This led directly to the creation of the 'Council of The Boys' Brigade' which launched the embryo movement. By October 1885 there were 15 BB companies.[83] It is interesting to note that many of these were run in conjunction with branches of the GFBRS. Perhaps the decision of the latter to allow the phasing out of uniform and drill from the 1870s was already being regretted. Certainly, candid comments published in the 'Foundry Boy' Magazine of the Wellington Palace Branch, throughout 1886 suggest that the new Boys' Brigade may have been exposing some of the weaknesses in the elder organisation. One contributor complained that, *'There is a want both in the Branch and in the Society of that "esprit de corps" that used to characterise the Society's workers.'* [84] There was also evidence that some of the 'Brigade' methods were being taken up again: *'Swimming and Drill classes are also formed and supply a healthy and invigorating discipline...'.* [85] Solutions for boys' meetings on the Sabbath were still being sought: *'Can anyone devise a means of lessening noise in the Forenoon Meeting?'* [86] In November, the faultfinder wrote again, *'... I find that the discipline in some of the branches is very lax in the matter of the children's conduct while assembling. I have seen the young people coming romping into the meeting hall, as if it were a playground, sitting down on their seats in the rudest manner possible, quarrelling and laughing and talking and generally behaving in a manner which shocks one who reverences the Sabbath because his Bible tells him so...'* [87] It was also stated in the same month, that a Club for senior lads' had begun, on Friday evenings from 7.30 - 9.45 with dominoes and other games, a conversation lounge, reading room and library. Consequently, the particular status and importance attributed by the founder of the BB to the promotion of habits of 'reverence and discipline' comes as no surprise.

The founding of The Boys' Brigade did not mean the end of the GFBRS. Far from it, as in 1886 membership was to peak at over 18,000 [16,000 boys & girls and 2,000 leaders]. [88] In 1925, there were still some 69 branches operating in Glasgow, 33 in outlying parts of Scotland and others in England and overseas. [89] By 1870, more than 70,000 copies of a book of Hymns and Psalms it produced had been sold or distributed. [90] The cover was adorned by an anchor and rope, a symbol adopted in 1885 by the BB as its emblem.[N] The emblem of the GFBRS was the open Bible with a lamp. Both elements would be adopted by brigades at the end of the century: the lamp by the Girls' Guildry and the open Bible by the Baptist Boys' Brigade in the USA.

There was a great similarity of organisational routine and practice between the GFBRS and The Boys' Brigade. Attention to detail at the regular meetings was paramount. As mentioned above, at camp and on excursions the senior GFBRS worker was given the title 'Captain'. [91] Boys were divided into groups of about eight under the charge of a 'monitor' who would look after them and check on attendance etc., a role very much like the one Smith gave to the Non-Commissioned Officers in his Boys' Brigade. Foundry boys were encouraged to give money to those less fortunate and to help to spread the mission work of the church and organisation. A small collecting box was issued, for regular donations, a system which was to become extensively used throughout the Boys' Brigade.

The close connection between the GFBRS and the origins of the Boys' Brigade were revealed by Mr James Scott Hunter, the son of the co - founder of the GFBRS, James Hunter. Scott Hunter had been a member of the BB as a boy, a significant fact given the work of his father, and was consequently a great admirer of the Brigade. He had also been associated with the Brigade as a young man (see photo. page 123). However, in an open letter published in 'The Foundry Boy in Action' magazine in November 1953 and addressed to Mr G.

'A small collecting box was issued for regular donations...'

Stanley Smith, Brigade Secretary of The Boys' Brigade, he made a most forth-right statement in reply to some of the 'history' he found printed in the 1953 BB Diary. His statement was in reply to an assertion that BB boys should be, '...proud to be members of the Pioneer Organisation for Boys'. Writing as the son of the founder of one organisation to the son of the founder of another, Hunter clearly viewed the Boys' Brigade to be undeniably the progeny of the GFBRS, which had been formed in 1865. He stated that the Boys' Brigade adopted the Foundry Boy uniform along with its role in having a drilled, disciplined organisation where boys were, '... in everyway, taught to acknowledge Almighty God'. In conclusion, Mr Scott Hunter stated: 'Your magnificent organisation sir, is just 18 years too late to hold the proud title of Pioneer.' Corrections to the Boys' Brigade's history, he asserted, should be made 'in due course'. Mr Scott Hunter whilst clearly an 'Old Boy' was only aged 76 years in 1953, although he had met William Smith 'seventy years ago' according to his letter. It is quite possible that his date of 1882 for the discontinuation of uniform by the Foundry Boys may be open to question, but the contemporary pictures of boys and the objects of the Society as we know them today, coincide exactly with Mr Scott Hunter's obser-vations.[92] Into the late 1950s and beyond BB Diaries would, nevertheless, con-tinue to state, 'The Boys' Brigade is the pioneer uniformed organisation for Boys...'

9

remained in the Hall till the chafed spirits of the lads were hushed again. When I reached the camp in the morning no traces of the disturbance remained.

The day opened with bright sunshine, so we determined to visit the Strachur encampment. Breakfast was hurried over with alacrity, lunch was packed, two large boats, one accomodating 110 and the other 60 were hired, and about 10.30 we set out for Strachur. Our boat had the advantage of a sail; so when we were clear of the shore, the sail was run up and we dashed along merrily. The lads were immensely pleased and their good humour was constantly bubbling over in snatches of songs, choruses and jokes. A little after noon we beached our boat and when the other boat came up we bathed and divided our lunch. Then like giants refreshed we set off to the Strachur encampment, and were met at the head of the avenue by Mr J. R. Sandilands one of the captains of the Strachur encampment. We found our friends in a state of high excitement. The Inveraray encampment of 150 girls had also come over to visit them and the whole company were joining in games in a large recreation field. Most of the girls found amusements to their own taste, and I noticed that some of more mature years, indulged in a little flirtation. No sooner did our contingent of lads appear on the field

than they threw down the gauntlet to the Strachur lads, challenging them to a trial at rounders, football, cricket or in fact anything. A few opponents at football presented themselves but were speedily disposed of, and the victors went whooping around the field crying like Alexander the Great for more to conquer. The monitors of course joined freely in the games and I enjoyed a good turn at Rounders. After several hours amusement we fed our company and at 5 p.m. we set off on our return journey. We were anxious now to get home, for a dark heavy cloud gathered, and we were still an hour and a half from home. When we were about the middle of the loch the rain which had long threatened came down in torrents. The lads took it all in perfect good humour, they huddled together as well as they could and chatted, laughed and sang as merrily as before. The breeze was good and brought us to land about 6.15. and immediately our company scampered off to the hall, hung up their jackets to dry and engaged in various games till tea was ready. After tea we had just time to recount our experiences leisurely; then we had evening worship and retired to rest before 10. We monitors found time for a brief chat together and we enjoyed the luxury.

A page from 'The Foundry Boy' magazine,
Wellington Palace Branch 1886

Even today, it is not uncommon for locally produced literature and websites to commence their history section with the words: *'The Boys' Brigade was the first uniformed organisation for boys.'*

CHAPTER FIVE

Shoe-blacks, Industrial Brigades and Training Ships

The Shoe-black Brigades

It was the evening of November 28th 1850, John MacGregor, John R. Fowler, R. James Snape and Francis S. Reilly, four Ragged School teachers on their way home from a meeting at the Field Lane school, were walking arm-in-arm up the middle of Holborn Hill in London. They were returning from a discussion on the need to create employment for the ragged boys of London knowing that the forthcoming Great Exhibition would soon attract thousands of foreign visitors to London. The friends had not walked far when the idea occurred to one them of 'making some of their boys' into Shoe-blacks similar to those often encountered in European and American cities. Before the walk ended they had estimated that it would take 10 shillings to equip a boy with a box, set of brushes and some kind of uniform. Each immediately pledged that sum.[93] It was John MacGregor, a committee member of the Ragged School Union, who took the initiative by persuading Lord Ashley (subsequently better known as Lord Shaftesbury), President of the Union, to publicly donate £5. Soon after, a public meeting was held to launch the shoe- black project. The boys would be employed during the day at fixed stations and overlooked by a paid superintendent. In the evening they would attend the night school from which they had been recommended whilst continuing to live with parents or relatives. In true Victorian style a committee was formed with John MacGregor as Chairman and Lord Ashley as President. The Shoe-black Society was now in business.

The first experimentation took place on 19th January 1851 in an alley off John Street close by the Strand. This involved committee members frequently running off to get a splash of mud on their boots from nearby street puddles in order to provide the required practice for the boys! By March 31st five young-sters were ready and it was time for the first public demonstration outside the National Gallery which despite some initial teething troubles proved a great success. Even though Costermongers called them 'Red Republicans', [94] arrangements were soon made with the police and an Act of Parliament was quickly passed to provide the boys with legal protection against being charged with begging or loitering. All was in place for May 1st 1851 when the Great Exhibition opened. The Shoe-black Brigade made quite an impression and the boys were kept constantly busy. Significant press coverage was given to their presence and to cap it all 'Punch' made good-natured fun of it all.

'Rob Roy'
John MacGregor and his 'Rob Roy' Canoe

The first 'Brigade' of shoe-blacks, originally based in Off Alley, near Charing Cross, wore bright red coats or jerseys, waterproof caps, black aprons and numbered badges. On July 30th 1851 MacGregor, always a showman, took thirty-three of the boys, in their blazing uniforms, and marched them through the Great Exhibition, thereby obtaining much public attention and sympathy for their work.[95] During the Exhibition the boys cleaned an estimated 101,000 pairs of boots, [96] quoted as 51,000 by Leapman, [97] and in the process raised over £500. Each member at the end of the day's work returned to headquarters. Sixpence was kept for dinner and the rest divided equally into three parts. One was retained by the boy, another was kept by the Society and the third was banked in the boy's name for future use. Different cleaning stations invariably attracted varying incomes. As an incentive, boys were placed in 'divisions', in effect 'classes', and good behaviour led to promotion to a higher division that offered access to the more profitable pitches. As more brigades were established the original Brigade became known as the 'Central Red' Brigade. Average earnings for boys by 1862 were in the region of seven shillings a month. The Central Brigade remained the most profitable. There boys could earn up to £25 per year. [98] Ragged Schools were closely allied to the Shoe-black Brigades and this encouraged many notable educational pioneers such as Quintin Hogg to become involved in their work.[99] & [(X)] MacGregor's lifelong friend and staunch

From a Photograph   wered by R. TAYLOR.
John MacGregor

co-worker Martin Ware was secretary of the Central Brigade for many years, and was in charge during its period of greatest activity 1851 to 1871. However, the dominant figure throughout was John MacGregor, well-connected, trained as a Barrister, and a great exponent of 'muscular Christianity', it was his vision fulfilled. As Hodder explained, the Brigade, '...was his hobby, his pet idea; he loved it and he loved every member of the Brigade, rough, uncouth, and almost brutal, as some of them were in their original state'. [100]

As an evangelistic Christian, the reason for John MacGregor's motivation is clear. It is useful, however, to examine his methodology which was evidently another key to his great success. He was able to view the children of the streets not as isolated wandering 'Arabs', but as what we would know today as a 'sub-culture'. A journalist in 1855 recorded much the same point: *'Street boys, indeed, are a distinct species of the human family'.*[101] Success with the Shoe-black Brigade idea made MacGregor sought after for advice as to how to combat the growing rate of juvenile delinquency. Still only twenty- seven years of age, he was providing information for a Government Select Committee on Criminal and Destitute Juveniles.[102] He was quick to impress upon the Committee that the uniform with numbered badge was very important to all who had dealings with the boys, ranging from the other non-uniformed boot-blacks to the local police. Uniforms, he went on to suggest, were also important as they provided a boy with an sense of 'esprit de corps', a clear identification which would act as a substitute for the boy's former street community. James Winter in *'London's Teeming Streets 1830 -1914'* [103] says that MacGregor would have been glad to second a famous and oft used and cited pronouncement by Boys' Brigade enthusiast Professor Henry Drummond. On one occasion in an address to Harvard University students in 1893, Drummond stated that there was no point in trying to use conventional inducements or techniques on, *'…these ragamuffins, as we call them - young roughs who have nobody else to look after them… You get a dozen boys together, and instead of forming them into a class, you get them into some little hall and put upon every boy's head a little military cap that costs in our country something like twenty cents, and you put around his waist a belt that costs about the same sum, and you call him a soldier. You tell him, "Now Private Hopkins, stand up. Hold up your head. Put your feet together." And you can order that boy about until he is black in the face, just because he has a cap on his head and a belt around his waist.'* [104] MacGregor, a very keen Volunteer Officer, and, according to Winter, only Lord Elcho could have been more dedicated, [105] valued the obedience and willingness to be ordered about enshrined in the Volunteer movement. To him, controlling the young was simply a means to an end, and that end was not just for Queen, country, empire or social peace. He wanted to create stalwart individuals, Protestant Christian soldiers ready to march as to war against, *'… idleness, dissipation and vice.'* [106] If another Volunteer Officer, William A. Smith, had written this some thirty two years later, no-one would have been surprised.

Following the success of what was to become the Central Red Brigade (which soon became self-supporting) others were rapidly formed. Like subsequent brigades, the shoe-blacks were soon 'split' on religious grounds. The Society of St. Vincent de Paul, for example, adopted the same model for Roman

John MacGregor's original sketch for the first Circular of the Ragged School Shoe-black Society - 1851

Pictures of Shoe-blacks appeared in many journals and magazines

Catholic boys operating in London's West End. Its official badge, 'S.V.P', embroidered on the arm of the bright blue and red uniform, caused some of the elder lads to suggest that it meant *'Shoes Vell Polished'* [107] Each London Brigade had its own colour, for example: East London - Blue; South London - Yellow; South Suburban - Red with Green facings. [108] Amongst the other brigades were those of Plymouth (founded 1853), Birmingham (1858), Glasgow (1865) and Edinburgh (1867). Numbers in each varied, but we know that in 1864 there were 373 boys working in eight Brigades in London. In 1881, there were some 320 boys in five Brigades. [109] Little is known regarding the numbers involved in individual units, but all the evidence points to them having a high turnover of membership. During 1857 and 1858 the numbers suggest that in London alone nearly 4,000 boys were found paid positions by the Brigade, initially as shoe-blacks, prior to moving onwards and upwards to other employment.

The wider informal education represented by membership of a shoe-black brigade would become most apparent in the final decades of the nineteenth century, but there was more than simply uniform, religion and discipline even in the earlier days of the movement. In July 1863, ten members of the London Shoe-black Brigade camped under canvas alongside members of the Norfolk Administrative Battalion of the Volunteers in their camp at Ganton-park, the seat of Lord Suffield.[110]

Between the 1870s and 1880s the whole purpose, nature and focus of the shoe-black brigade work changed. In brief, as these decades progressed free full-time elementary education for all was introduced and the number of jobs available to young people expanded. By the end of this period the brigades had set down a pattern, clearly recognisable in the organisations which were to follow. As Montague notes:

'The conditions of London labour having so changed, the object of these societies is changed also. The aim is now to provide discipline and instruction for those who are getting their living in the streets and who, but for these societies, would have no instruction or control at all.' [111]

A home was built for the Central Red Brigade in 1874 in Great Saffron Hill, Farringdon Street with sleeping accommodation for 44. It also contained a schoolroom, bath, coffee-room and gymnasium. Non-residential boys returned home at night.[112] The Shoe-black Brigade was evolving in a way that those looking back on the success story of The Boys' Brigade would easily recognise.

John MacGregor's Brigade Boys

Lord Guthrie, Boys' Brigade President and son of Rev. Thomas Guthrie an Edinburgh Pioneer of work with young people, writing to The Times, on the 9th February 1915, summed up the reasons for its popularity:

'Boys of the working class are not to be held for any length of time on drill alone. They work hard during the day, and the training needs to be recreational and attractive as well as instructive.' [113]

To understand just how they had evolved by the 1880s it is helpful to look at the evolution of one society. Fortunately, the minute book of the West London (Purple) Brigade between 1885 and 1902 has survived.[114] This Brigade was founded in 1857 and by 1885 was based at 57 Bessborough Place, Pimlico where 46 boys were in residence. The whole operation was church-run. Initially, the Revd. Samuel Martin, and later the Revd. Henry Simon, of Westminster Chapel, Buckingham Gate, took responsibility for 'supervising' the work of the unit. Both ensured religious instruction was dispensed every Sunday. By the 1880s stands for the boys were being rented. For instance, the annual fee for three spots inside the terminus of London Brighton and South Coast Railway station cost £25. Even at that price, however, they were deemed a sound investment. A gymnasium was provided in 1886. This proved so successful that an instructor was recruited from the Brigade of Guards and dumb bells and clubs purchased for £3. 16s 3d. Regular Old Boys meetings were held, sometimes involving entertainment. There was a fife and drum band for which a Bandmaster was paid £8 7s 6d. Uniforms were provided consisting of tunics and caps, along with brass badges. The Society arranged for some boys to emigrate to Canada where they were employed on farms. Each year an 'annual treat' was organised. In 1887, the destination was Hastings. Stripes - one, two or three - were awarded for good conduct and prizes given for the best performers in the gymnasium, for musical drill, singing or recitations. Boys were encouraged to put on displays to provide entertainment and raise funds. In 1890, a complaint was made by a Miss Webb of 267 Vauxhall Bridge Row concerning the noise made by the Society's Band passing her house early in the morning en route to embarkation for its annual excursion. The managers agreed to make no response. A note is made of the presentation of a *'handsome Bible to the Brigade.'* Sometimes lads too, would be presented with a Bible upon leaving the Brigade.

Some thirty five years after the initial formation of Shoe-black Brigades and more than forty years on from the start of the Ragged School Union there was evidently still much work to be done. The 1880s was the decade of the Boys' Brigade, but it was simply a part of a growing provision for young people. The June 1886 Manchester Conference of Ragged School teachers which took place in the Central Refuge Hall, Strangeways, featured a number of speakers outlining what was being done for poor children. Mr R. B. Taylor described the work of the Central Refuge, the Working Boys' Homes, and Girls' Home, and the Training Ship - all dealing with cases of destitution and homelessness of those over ten years of age. The meeting adjourned to the City Mission Hall for tea and further conference. *'Mr Kirlew explained other branches of the Refuge work - such as the Industrial Brigades, Caxton Brigades, and Messenger Brigades, Boys' Lodging House, Children's Shelter and the Camp at Llandudno.'* [112]

A Caxton Brigade boy

The Caxton Brigade operated in a number of cities and was started in Strangeways Manchester as part of the Boys' and Girls' Refuges and Children's Aid Society. Books and tracts specially printed and published by the Boys' Industrial Brigades, based at 1, Clarence St. Manchester, were sold by the Brigade boys. A typical book was *'Daddy's Bobby a Tale of Manchester Street Life'*. Just as the 'Big Issue' today is an attempt to elevate its sellers into working life, so it was with the publications of the Caxton Brigade. In 1886, the year of the first Boys' Brigade Camp, the Seaside Camp of the Boys' and Girls' Refuges had been operating for two years, [116] and unlike the first BB Camp, in a Church Hall, this Camp was under canvas, *'...but we also have a Camp for City Boys at Llandudno, which is intended for street boys of from, say 12 to 16 years of age, who may not be really poorly, but who need a holiday. We wish you could see this camp. It is in a field near the shore, and there are eight bell-tents, where military order and discipline are kept up. All the cooking, etc, is done by the boys, and they enjoy the camp life immensely.'* [117]   Evidently, in 1886 the 108 boys marched to camp in groups, as the following story relates: *'It is amusing to hear the remarks of some of the boys who go to Camp. The other Saturday, as a little group marched from the railway station to the Camp, one boy having his cap off for a few minutes only, his companion said to him, "Oh Billy you are getting red!" We need hardly say the face had not yet lost the sallow complexion of our Manchester alleys.'* [118]

One of the earliest forms of Industrial Brigade, other than the Shoe-blacks, was that of the House Boys' Brigade. This grew out of an idea originated by Lady Wolverton, the mother of the Bishop of Peterborough, who was well known for her interest in helping the poor. Her initial idea was a *'Doorstep Brigade'* so-called because the cleaning of doorsteps was the first employment taken up by the lads. A Home was established for them at 18, Lower Sloan Street, Chelsea with a first intake of seventeen boys, ten of whom returned to their own homes to sleep. Door knockers were also polished by the boys and eventually many other household duties were performed. Eventually the name was changed to the *'House Boys' Brigade'* which, in 1872, extended its work by breaking into three separate Brigades. One was located at 146, Marylebone Road, another at Ebury Street and a third at St. Mary Abbott's Kensington. [119]

The Kensington Brigade was situated at 7, Church Street and was superintended by a Mr. Vine and his wife who took on the role of matron. This institution was typical in that it had The Right Hon. Lord Alverstone as an active vice-president, the Vicar as chairman and a Lt. Colonel as Hon. Secretary. Another member of the clergy acted as Chaplain. There was a Mr. W. Collier who acted as schoolmaster, and a committee formed from ladies and gentlemen of the district. A Band of Hope and Sunday School were organised as well as a special Bible Class for the elder boys. In her article in 'Home Words' (1909) [120] Marion Leslie outlined the object of the Brigade: '...*to train and educate destitute boys and to teach them useful work by which they can earn their own living when they leave the Home...* .' The Kensington Brigade only received boys of 'known good character'. It was not an institution for waifs and strays, but for ' *... the deserving class of respectable boys rendered destitute by the loss of their parents, or who are dependent on a widowed mother.'* Destitute boys were admitted between 12 and 14 years of age with a minimum height of 4ft 5in., in good health and not of known bad character. The work was said to make the boys muscular and healthy and able to learn the habits of punctuality and industry. Normally boys lived-in for three years. Old boys meetings were held each year and an annual camp was organised at Hythe. Marks were awarded for such virtues as good behaviour, cleanliness, punctuality as well as Bible knowledge and outdoor sports with prizes being awarded at the end of each year. The boys were given ten per cent of their weekly earnings, viz: five per cent as pocket money (paid weekly) and five per cent put into a bank account for the boys' future. The earnings of the boys rendered the home virtually self-supporting.

Working as a 'House Boy' was not always good for the boys. A report from 'The Times' of Wednesday October 18th 1882 [121] reported an Inquest at the Middlesex Hospital relating to the death of William Collins, aged 15, who had been a member of the House Boys' Brigade at 146, Marylebone Road. William died from injuries received due to falling from a window at the residence of Mr. W. Stafford Northcote. A witness reported seeing William falling from the fifth storey where he had been cleaning windows. An iron rail on which he had been leaning had given-way and he had fallen 50ft on to the doorstep. The Jury returned a verdict of 'Accidental Death'. Mr. Chevens representing the Brigade, added that he had given orders that none of the boys should in future be engaged in window-cleaning.

Today, very little remains of the House Boys' Brigades but, remarkably, the splendid headquarters building of one of them still exists. The 'Pimlico House-Boy Brigade' originally based at 147, 151 and 153 Ebury Street, London SW, became 'Incorporated' and moved premises around 1900 into the 'Silver and Gold-Plating Works' 31, Elizabeth Street SW. The 'Superintendent' Mr J. H. Kirby changed his designation to 'Resident Secretary and Manager' at about the same time as the move. The Brigade was still operating in 1910, even providing a service for charging motor batteries! [122]

The Kensington House Boys' Brigade.

A Novel Parish Organization.
By MARION LESLIE.

Smart Page Boys earn a shilling an hour.

The header from the 1909 article in 'Home Words'

Pimlico House-Boy Brigade,

J. H. KIRBY,
Resident Secretary and Manager.

INCORPORATED

Silver and Gold-Plating Works.

Office:—*31*, ELIZABETH STREET, S.W.

c.2005

c.1905

PIMLICO. HOUSE. BOY. BRIGADE LONDON.   F.K.S.1231.

Two Scottish Industrial Brigades: the work of David Harris in Edinburgh and William Quarrier in Glasgow

It was 1867 before the concept of providing an Industrial Brigade arrived in Edinburgh. David Harris aimed to do something for those too old for a Ragged School (i.e. leavers) and the scheme would be self-supporting.[123] Clothing and dormitories would be provided, *'...to counter the evil effects of city life'.* At its first meeting on 4th October 1867 Sheriff Watson, a pioneer of the Ragged School movement in Scotland chaired the gathering.[124] There were many destitute and homeless youngsters in Edinburgh struggling to raise themselves. Harris saw the idea of 'Shoe-blacks' as good examples of what might be done. Reminiscent of the founders of the original Shoe-black brigade sixteen years earlier, Harris felt ashamed that visitors came to Edinburgh to see the tourist sights and then spied, *'...a struggling mass of youthful depravity.'* He identified the need for a 'missing link' after Ragged Schools and before regular work was obtained. In his opinion the Brigade would give the boy, *'...respect and reliance for himself.'*

The Brigade scheme looked to Europe, the United States and Australia for inspiration regarding Newspaper Sales-boys which did not exist in Edinburgh, to consider apprenticeships, messengers and even tourist guides. Surprisingly golf caddies were also a possible local option. Three Brigades emerged: Shoe-black, Messenger and Industrial. Harris was aware that a Superintendent, who must be a Christian, would need to be appointed to supervise evenings and teach. He was concerned that they could spawn what he called, 'educated devils'. No doubt referring to Arthur Wellesley, The Duke of Wellington's comment: *'Educate people without religion and you make them but clever devils.'* The three R's would be taught at night with games the rest of the time. Boys would contribute towards their food from their earnings.

On the 4th November 1867 the Street Arabs of Edinburgh were invited to a house in Cockburn Street and 57 of them turned up, tempted by the 'tea and cookies' on offer. All the lads were miserably clad, most of them in rags, covered

Just off the street

with filth and vermin, and all of them extraordinarily hungry. After hymns and prayers and short speeches, some fifteen of them were induced to take up residence in the home. The boys were found work as shoe-blacks, farm workers, messengers and apprentices, but the first year proved to be an eventful one due to the *'wild natures, ungoverned passions and roving dispositions of the lads.'* W. J. Gordon provides some detail of the escapades of the first residents:...

'Cases of boys absconding with their wages and selling their clothes, staying out all night, and being hauled in by their chums with the aid of blankets let down from the windows, were not uncommon. On one occasion their blacking-boxes were piled up against the entrance door of the Home, so that when the superintendent opened it, instead of admitting the boys, he received a shower of black-ing-boxes about his ears. On another occasion the superintendent unfortunately left a large barrel of coals in the lobby. The boys, taking advantage of this, kept firing volley after volley of coals at the door, and it was not until eight o'clock, when their ammuni-tion was well-nigh reduced to dross, that the siege was raised and the superintendent effected his escape. This was no easy matter. Armed with the barrel lid as a shield, he at last succeeded in running the gauntlet. The boys beat a hasty retreat, singing at the pitch of their voices, 'Scots wha hae'. One day our young friends decamped in a body to Glasgow, leaving the Home empty!'

The experiences of the first year caused the Home to move to new prem-ises in Leith Street Terrace where the work was properly begun. Later, there was a further expansion to 72, Grove Street, Fountainbridge. Between 1868 and 1900 there were some 4,000 inmates.[125] The boys wore no uniforms so they would not be singled-out as 'charity boys' and every effort made for them to train as skilled artisans. In 1887, among the 130 boys in the Brigade there were joiners, brass-finishers, tailors, lithographers, saddle-makers, blacksmiths, printers, glaziers, plumbers, bookbinders, tinsmiths, wire-workers, and drafts men. The facilities at the Home, in 1888, included a large dining hall, spacious dormitories, kitchen, store-room, school room, meeting room, gymnasium and a large sized swimming bath. One of the Rules of the home stated that every boy was obliged to attend the Brigade Sunday School at 9.30 a.m. and the Brigade Sunday evening service at 7, as well as a place of public worship on Sunday forenoon. Attendance at the Home service in the afternoon at 2 o'clock was optional.

Towards the end of November 1864, William Quarrier, on his way home from his shoe-making business in Glasgow, encountered a small ragged boy who was in tears because the matches he had been selling had been stolen. William, seeing in the lad a reflection of himself when he was a very poor young boy and experienced similar misery, was moved to help him. However, upon reflection, William was spurred into widening his benevolence to include all such boys in Glasgow. He sent a letter to the Glasgow Herald which was published on December 2nd. In that he recounted his observations of the London Shoe-black Brigade, made on his occasional visits to the metropolis, and how much such an institution would benefit Glasgow. *'Always on my return to Glasgow... I have wished that we had such an institution here'*, he commented. Fortunately there was some support for his scheme, notably from Lord Provost Blackie, the head of the well-known publishing house. A Committee was formed and £100 raised to make a start. The first action was to let the lads know what was planned for them and some forty or fifty boys appeared for a *'gran' tea in a gentleman's hoose'*, that gentleman being William Quarrier and his house being in Kingston Place. At the great tuck-in, Quarrier explained about the Shoe-black Brigade, its uniform and the kit with which they would be provided: a peaked cap, navy-blue flannel jacket trimmed with red, a red badge on the arm and dark trousers, a box of brushes and blacking. Eight pence from every shilling earned would be kept and the other four-pence used for clothing, etc.. Attendance at a night school was expected, as was Sunday school attendance. There followed two immediate disappointments as just fourteen of the boys expressed an interest in joining the Brigade that night and a number of family articles went missing from the house!

Eventually, the Shoe-black Brigade numbered 200, all wearing its distinctive uniform. Headquarters moved from Jamaica Street via Bath Street to 114

Trongate where there was space for some twenty or thirty boys to live-in. For many people this success would be enough, but just after he set up the Shoe-black Brigade, Quarrier turned his attention to the young newspaper vendors and organised a News Brigade on similar lines to that of the Shoe-blacks. Within a year of the Shoe-black Brigade, a third group, the Parcels Brigade was introduced. These lads, wearing a uniform of canvas tunic, black belt and a special badge offered to carry parcels for the citizens at the rate of 2d for a half-mile and 3d a mile. By 1868, the Trongate premises had become the headquarters of all three brigades and was known as 'The Industrial Brigade Home'. The Brigade work continued for the remainder of the century, but William Quarrier proceeded to institute refuges, missions and homes in the city and beyond, helped by influential friends such as the famous evangelist D.L. Moody. Each year, from 1872, Quarrier produced a report or 'Narrative of Facts' as he termed it, describing the activities of the various Children's Homes. In a number of these publications thanks are offered to the Foundry Boys Society for the practical help given. Remarkably, until 1882, William was still running his business although he had been selling it off since the late 1870s.[126]

In Rev. Urquhart's 'Life Story of William Quarrier', the tale is recounted of

David Grey cleans the boots of William Quarrier

David Grey, one of the original lads who joined the Shoe-black Brigade. He had been one of the wildest on Glasgow's streets. Swearing, cursing and fighting was his life whilst gambling was his passion. He had even pawned his clothes, having only the rags in which he stood up. He was 15 years old when he became one of 'Quarrier's Boys'. David Grey, however, managed to overcome his addiction and became the smartest brusher of boots the Brigade ever had. He could earn as much as thirty shillings a week. An amateur artist who begged a sitting of Mr Quarrier and one of his boys, was allowed to produce a

painting of the great philanthropist having his boots cleaned by David Grey. Unfortunately that work was, within a short time, regarded as a memorial to the young man. Grey had gone to sea about a year after joining the Brigade. After each voyage he would return with some small memento for Mr and Mrs Quarrier, the best friends he had ever had. On one occasion, however, instead of the usual visit the news came of his death on a foreign shore.[127]

The Orphan Homes of Scotland at Bridge-of-Weir, founded by Quarrier and known as 'Quarrier's Homes' ran its own Boys' Brigade Company from 1906. The Home's very successful BB Coy was the 2nd Bridge of Weir and the Captain was the headmaster of the school, Mr J. Gordon Kennedy. The Company number was changed during the inter-war period to the 1st Bridge of Weir.

Training Ships

Another of the ideas to extend Ragged School work in the second half of the 19th century, particularly for those of the older age range of 13 - 16 years, was the provision of Training Ships. The idea of boys being given naval training was not new. In 1756, Sir John Fielding a London author and magistrate collected together a number of urchins who had been brought before him and had them sent to serve on HMS Barfleur.[128] The 'Marine Society' founded by Joseph Hanway at the outbreak of the Seven Years' War was established as a 'recruiting' response to the shortage of volunteers for the Navy and was requested by Fielding to take boys he sent to them. Although having taken some 5,174 boys from its inception, at the end of the war it turned its attentions solely towards younger recruits. An Act of Parliament in 1772, by which it became 'Incorporated', allowed it to apprentice poor boys to the royal and merchant services. In 1786, the Society commissioned the first pre-sea training ship in the world, the 'Beatty', moored off Deptford, to provide a regular supply of trained boys. Thirty boys lived on board where they were educated and supervised by a schoolmaster, superintendent, mate, boatswain and cook. After several years, the Admiralty lent the Society a new vessel. In 1862, the Society was lent the first of a number of vessels named 'Warspite'.

With the navy being of such national importance and the provider of so many jobs, life aboard ship was considered to be a very good training, and not only for a possible future career. The navy was also very popular amongst teenage boys. No doubt, the choice of an anchor emblem for the Boys' Brigade, by William Smith, was not co-incidental it was, *'…an attractive and subtle choice'.* [129] Some of the vessels used for 'training', however, could only be described as 'hulks', no longer under sail, whilst others were very much more seaworthy, providing a full range of nautical activities. Not all the 'ships' were actually on the sea, with some being described as 'Land Ships, being specially constructed on land to resemble sailing vessels. The reasons for boys being on these ships varied from them simply being destitute to being referred there by the magistrates.

A typical training ship was the 'Chichester' moored at Greenhithe which from 18th December 1866, took-in 50 homeless boys from a refuge at Parker Street near Covent Garden. It was obtained and administered by the 'National Refuges for Destitute Children' which was run by Lord Shaftesbury. The second ship, the Arethusa, was bought after £5,000 had been donated to the society by Angela Burdett-Coutts in 1873. The Arethusa was opened on 3rd August 1874, and some 250 *'poor boys of good character'* were provided with uniforms and began training on board. One of the ships, the 'Havanah', on shore near Cardiff which housed 57 boys from 1861, even ran its own Shoe-black Brigade. The 'Worcester', based at Erith had 130 boys aged 12 - 15 years under training from 1862.

In Liverpool, the 'Indefatigable' from 1865 housed 60 destitute boys, the 'Clarence' was a reformatory ship for 194 Roman Catholic boys which operated from 1863 and the 'Akbar' from 1865 took on 195 reformatory boys. Also in the Mersey was 'HMS Conway', perhaps one of the most famous of the training ships, which from 1859 trained officers for the Merchant Navy under the auspices of the Mercantile Marine Service Association and was the first of three ships to bear the name as school ships.[130] The gold medal awarded annually by Queen Victoria to the 'finest sailor' of the 100 boys on this ship was the inspi ration for one of the earliest service awards in the Church Lads' Brigade.[131]

The Akbar was run by the Liverpool Juvenile Reformatory Association which proved to be: '*...one of the most go-ahead in the country*'.[132] The Association had been established following the Youthful Offenders' Act of 1854, which recognised youthful offenders as a separate group. Typically, detention in the Akbar was not intended as a punishment, the boys, aged between 12 and 16 years, already having served a short prison sentence. The idea was that the time served on board, usually three years, would inculcate discipline and provide training that would be beneficial in later years. Although life was quite harsh on the ship, boys were usually happy to favourably balance the positive aspects against the negatives. For instance, boys would leave the ship to go on shore and rarely attempt to escape, even when left alone. The biggest problem with shore leave was that the boys were often met with a barrage of coarse jokes and jeers from those they encountered. On Sundays the boys attended the Floating Church in Birkenhead where, '*... their conduct is spoken of by the superintendent in terms of commendation*'.[133] A band was formed in 1858 and regularly performed in Birkenhead. The boys' uniform consisted of blue trousers, guernseys and caps for every day. The caps were replaced by glazed hats when they manned the boats, attended church or assembled on the deck for official inspections. In 1878, Benjamin Blower, author of the book 'The Mersey' wrote about the Akbar:

'*Instead of being confined to the cells of a prison, here are 160 lads, of the age of twelve and upwards, undergoing the most close and vigilant supervision. Their habits are watched, their morals guarded, their minds cultivated, and their hands taught the useful trades of tailoring and shoemaking, their bodies are well fed and exercised by their being put through all the lessons of a seafaring apprenticeship, climbing masts, hoisting and lowering sails, taking in reefs etc.; and above all, their souls are cared for, being brought in daily contact with the lessons of God's Holy Word, and taught to sing the praises of Him whose name they had formerly been accustomed to dishonour and blaspheme.*'[134]

The landship 'Endeavour', based at Feltham from 1866 was another training establishment. The 'Cornwall' at Purfleet, a reformatory ship, was established in 1859 for 155 boys. The idea of using Training Ships to teach boys about life was to endure for many years. For instance, in 1888, the landship 'James Arthur' was constructed as a life-sized replica of a real ship to house and train 30 boys at the Quarrier's Orphan Homes of Scotland, Bridge of

Akbar and HMS Conway

Weir.[135] By the end of the 19th century along with Messenger and Shoe-black Brigades and Working Youth's Institutes, a 'Training Ship' was on the list of all self-respecting institutions aimed at young people. A good example, quoted in 'Sixty Years in Waifdom', was the Manchester and Salford Boys' and Girls' Refuges and Homes charity.[136] In 1869, the 'Cumberland' was taken over for use as a training vessel by the newly formed Clyde Industrial Training Ship Association. The Association had the object of providing for the education and training of boys who, through poverty, parental neglect, or any other cause were destitute, homeless, or in danger from association with vice or crime. In 1889, the Cumberland was destroyed by a fire and was replaced by the 'Empress', a wooden battleship originally known as HMS Revenge. Between 1870 and 1875, the Forest Gate School District operated a ship called the 'Goliath' moored on the Thames. It provided boys from all London's Poor Law authorities with training to help equip them to enter the Royal or Merchant Navy. In 1871 an article in 'The Times' [137] expounded the virtues of life aboard the ship:

'We are told, and we can well believe, that the training supplied on board the 'Goliath', -education not only in books, but in work, - transforms with astonishing rapidity and completeness even the facial and bodily characteristics of the street arabs who have the

good fortune to be drafted to the School Ship at Gravesend. Dull eyes brighten, narrow chests expand, stunted figures erect themselves, and the mental and moral nature partakes of the healthy change. In this metamorphosis we have a promise for the future. An addition of energy to the national life, an improvement of the physical type of the race, rescue of thousands from a life of squalor and dependence, - these are gains worth purchasing at a higher price than a few out-of-date wooden men-of-war.'

Although successful, the ship was destroyed by fire on 22nd December 1875 with the loss of twenty-three lives. In 1877, a replacement vessel, the 'Exmouth' took over the role and was then moored off Grays in Essex and managed by the Metropolitan Asylums Board. The 'Exmouth' had a companion ship, a brigantine called the 'Steadfast', used for cruising and to provide the boys with practical training in seamanship. The original 'Steadfast' was condemned in 1894 and replaced by a new vessel of the same name.[138]

In 1933, members of the 32nd Birmingham Company of The Boys' Brigade spent their week's annual Camp aboard the 'Implacable' a French wooden warship dating from 1800 and captured just after the battle of Trafalgar. Implacable had actually been used as a boys training ship between 1842 and 1908. As part of a 'crew' of 120 BB boys they spent the time diving, swimming, rowing, sailing, signalling and even playing water-polo. *'They slept in hammocks, washed and scrubbed the decks, saluted in memory of Nelson and pretended not to be "landlubbers"'*. [139] The Implacable, which lay in HM Dockyard, Portsmouth was run by a committee in order that city boys might 'taste the sea'. Whilst the boys on the nineteenth century Training Ships were never officially known as being members of 'Brigades', they were usually aged between 12 and 17 years, uniformed, often there voluntarily, drilled and subjected to strict discipline. Typical naval activities were designed to improve them physically and Bible teaching to improve them spiritually. Similar uniforms, discipline, physical training and spiritual guidance clearly continued into the twentieth century and beyond with organizations such as The Boys' Brigade.

CHAPTER SIX

Edinburgh Pioneers - Catherine Sinclair and John Hope

Catherine Sinclair and the 'Ulbster Juvenile Volunteers'

A tall Gothic monument stands on the corner of St. Colme Street and North Charlotte Street, near the western end of Queen Street, in Edinburgh. Described both as an 'Eleanor Cross' and 'Gothic Fountain' it is a memorial, designed by David Bryce, to Catherine Sinclair (1800 - 1864). Erected in 1867 it was given the following inscription in 1901: (O)

Catherine Sinclair's Gothic Monument

'She was the friend of all children and through her book 'Holiday House' speaks to them still.

Besides success in her writings, which were many and popular, she was an early pioneer in philanthropy, her Volunteer Brigade for the boys of Leith was the first of its kind. She initiated cooking depots for working men, and erected the first Drinking Fountain in Edinburgh. Her hall for lectures and her work among cabmen endeared her name to different sections of her fellow citizens. This monument was raised by some of her many friends, the inscription, except the name and dates, was added in 1901 by her affectionate nephew Sir Tollemache Sinclar Bart. of Ulbster Caithness-shire.'

Catherine was a remarkable individual. The daughter of Sir John Sinclair of Ulbster by his second wife and one of five sisters and two brothers, she was, like her siblings, over six feet tall - exceptional for the time

The Sinclair Fountain in Princes Street

- and must have cut quite a dash whilst performing her charitable work in the poorest districts of mid 19th century Edinburgh. She had, no doubt, inherited the idea of good works from her father who was a noted philanthropist. Besides her philanthropic endeavours she was the author of over forty books, some of which were 'big sellers'. Most were feminist texts or children's books packed full of 'natural youngsters'. The former reflected her political beliefs, the latter her famous wit and humour. In his publication *'A Book of Memories of Great Men and Women of the Age. From Personal Acquaintance'*.[140] S. C. Hall, who knew Catherine as a neighbour and friend when she stayed with her brother in Kensington, London, said of her: *'Religion assumed no ascetic character with Catherine Sinclair; she could be merry and wise, and was always cheerful; she was at times full of humour; some of her sayings, indeed, though thoroughly womanly, might be circulated as examples of pure wit.'* Hall also recounted that the steps that led to Catherine's house door in Edinburgh were known as 'The Giants' Causeway' because of the height of her family. Unfortunately her face although

Portraits of Catherine Sinclair
In her youth (inset)
and in the 1860s

quite handsome was pitted by small-pox. Hall stated that, *'She… needed no other beauty than that which is communicated to the features of the soul.'* From her earnings as a writer, and no doubt with some of her father's extensive wealth, she founded an Industrial School for the training of girls for domestic service, a mission station, pension schemes for the destitute elderly, cooking depots (canteens) for working people, public seating, drinking fountains and cabmen's shelters [141]. Her canteens alone were, in 1864, feeding 1,200 people a day [142].

It must have been in the latter months of 1860 that Catherine commenced one of her most innovative ventures following initial success with the training of girls in the Ulbster Mission Industrial School in the Water of Leith, an old village which had now become part of Edinburgh and was one of its poorer areas. This new initiative would be an evening school for boys linked with the formation of a corps of 'Juvenile Volunteers'. The idea for forming a Volunteer Corps for the boys may well have originated from all the publicity surrounding the great Royal Review of Scottish Volunteers by Queen Victoria when some 20,000 Volunteers paraded in August 1860. [143].

In a letter to Professor Blackie [144] undated, but probably written in the week commencing 21st April 1861, Catherine invited him to attend a special meeting at St. George's School which was at No. 10, Young Street, where she intended to present medals to the boys as a token of their enlistment into the corps she calls the 'Ulbster Volunteers'. Clearly she had overcome the first challenge; to tame their wild instincts in return for education, and must have been proud to show them off:

'Dear Sir,

If you could spare a few minutes on Friday evening to do a very good action, will you come any time between 7 and 8 to the Young Street School almost next door to you and say a few words of encouragement to above 100 ragged boys who will have signed their names to a request that I will give them an education. They range from 12 to 19 and are **wilder than panthers and as ignorant as the heathens,** *but they have espoused a united desire to be tamed and civilised. I have hired two soldiers to drill them and a Band Master to teach them singing and Military instruments - also a reading, 'riting and 'rithmetic master for the 3Rs. Next Friday I am leaving Scotland. I am to take leave of them by presenting medals as a token of their enlistment into "The Ulbster Volunteers" and I have promised that all those who conduct themselves well during the 5 months of my absence shall have a uniform. It occurred to me yesterday that if you would throw in a few words on the occasion they would be a great assistance therefore*

Young Street, Edinburgh in 2008
The site of the school (now occupied by a more
recent building) indicated by the arrow.

I boldly venture to make this request trusting to your kindness to excuse this impingement on your valuable time.

With best regards to Mrs Blackie.

Yours very truly,

CS'

Professor Blackie evidently made some of his valuable time available to the boys and the successful meeting was reported in the Edinburgh Evening Courant the following night; Saturday 27th April 1861. The paper outlined the formation of the corps:

'... composed of boys and lads belonging to the village of Water of Leith, and who have been embodied under the name of the "Ulbster Volunteers". The Company, numbering fully 100, assembled last night ... to hear the address of Professor Blackie and to receive medals from Miss Sinclair in token of their enrolment.'

'This excellent movement has arisen from the establishment by Miss Sinclair of the "Ulbster Mission School" intended to give the girls in the locality above-mentioned an industrial education. This school has been in existence for about 18 months and has been productive of much good. In order to do something for the boys of the district Miss Sinclair resolved also to commence an evening school for their benefit which is now open every night between 6 and 9 o'clock in Young Street School-room. The lads receive an excellent elementary education and two serjeants have been engaged to put them through military drill, in which they have made considerable progress although only a week or two has elapsed since they were brought together. We may also mention that a bandmaster has been engaged to instruct the youth in instrumental music.'

Catherine asked Prof. Blackie '*... to deliver them the medals as pledges of their enrolment in the noble regiment of Ulbster Volunteers.*' His speech was a eulogy for the Volunteer Movement:

'*The boy was not worth a snuff who did not make a great noise, but the thing was to be able to direct it to a good purpose ... In fact, they must all be soldiers, for if any man was to do any good he must be a soldier - (laughter) - he must behave in a certain way, and get his medal.*'

Then each got their medal, '*... as a badge of that noble fellowship into which they had enlisted themselves and as a recognition of their independence and their nobility in coming forward to be treated as reasonable beings and Christians.(Applause)*'

'*When she should come back from London in the course of a few months she would dress them in the garb of volunteers ... At this stage, one of the young lads was brought forward in the proposed uniform of the corps which consisted of a blue cloth tunic, braided with scarlet; a Glengarry bonnet, similarly braided; and knickerbockers.*'

The Volunteer Review Medal of 1860

The medal presented to each was , '*... one of the medals struck some time ago in commemoration of the great volunteer review in the Queen's Park - bearing on one side a profile of her Majesty with the date of the review and on the reverse the figure of a Highlander with the inscription "In defence"*'.[145]

This successful brigade of Christian boys initially referred to as the 'Ulbster Volunteers' was soon to become known as the 'Sinclair Cadet Company', or more formally as the 'Juvenile Corps of Ulbster Volunteers'. The reason for the introduction of the words 'cadet' and 'juvenile' into the name being due to the fact that a 'senior' corps for young men in the Water of Leith, inspired by the youngsters, was formed just a few months later. That senior Company enrolled as the No. 12 Company of the Edinburgh Rifle Regiment (Volunteers) or 'The Sinclair Volunteers' as they became known. According to Barclay, [146] [(P)] complete with band, they had, like the Juveniles, been raised at Catherine's own expense and had adopted her family crest (a star and ad astra virtus). There are references to this volunteer corps as having *'intelligent young men, chiefly artisans'* as members.[147] Almost identical to what would become the Boys' Brigade's clientele.

The Scotsman of 14th December 1861 praised the uniforms and related the story:

'... So rapidly did the boys improve in their drill that Miss Sinclair was induced to present them all with uniforms, and a fine appearance they present when going through their various evolutions in true military style. The men in the village determined to follow the example of the boys and formed themselves into a Volunteer corps.'

To arrive at a position of having a uniformed group worthy of being emulated by the older lads and young men, suggests that a transformation in the initial Juvenile Corps had evidently taken place during the year of 1861, particularly in respect of the original, rather unfavourable and uncouth 'raw material'. Very little survives to throw light upon just how this training was achieved in the weekly workings of the Corps, although the Drill Sgt., Mr. Edwards, seems to have played a significant role. The flute band of the Juvenile Corps also turned out on parade with the seniors. The Scotsman of 17th July 1861 (p.2,) reporting on a public meeting of the Water of Leith Volunteer Corps stated:

'The meeting was numerously attended, and was enlivened by the performances of the flute band in connection with the Ulbster Mission School and Juvenile Volunteer Corps, recently organised under the patronage of Miss Catherine Sinclair....Mr Edwards Drill Sgt I/C the Corps.'

Professor Blackie had become a key inspirational figure for both the Senior Volunteers and the Juvenile Corps and before the end of the year, probably around October, Catherine wrote to him: [148]

'*My Dear Professor Blackie,*

You have no idea of the anxiety felt by the Volunteers, for your appearance on the day they are to be enrolled, Friday next at 8 in the evening in the Assembly Rooms. I wished to change the day to suit you, but Mr Pakington had ? on purpose to be pres ent and I will address them also, but the constant remark is "It will be nothing without Professor Blackie." I trust you will not disappoint us, but come even if it were at 10 o'clock and we shall wait. There will be about 200 boys and men, all anxious for you to appear, as you will make many deserving persons happy and really they have exerted themselves, drilling every night for the last six months. Many are reformed characters and they have a reading room which I furnish with newspapers and books, draughts and solitaire which keeps them all from the public house. Your first appearance among the boys is often remembered and you would not know your old friends again now, in their civilized state.

I wish Mrs Blackie would join me at tea in the gallery where the guests are to have a quiet cup of tea. Serjeant Edwards is to call upon you for an answer tomorrow and I earnestly hope it may be favourable.

With best regards to Mrs Blackie and yourself.

Yours ever Truly,

CS'

In December 1861 Professor Blackie had returned, this time with the senior 'Sinclair Volunteers', now numbering some seventy plus, for their official swearing into office ceremony. [149] Needless to say, there were a number of speeches directed toward Catherine for her benevolence and initiative, and for those who were carrying out the work on a weekly basis. Prof. Blackie addressed the meeting on a classical theme, emphasising an 'imperative' need for drill at both school and university. He saw physical drill and training as being as important as training the mind:

'*There is nothing that tends so much both to brace the body and the mind, and to pre-vent us acquiring the narrow habits of mere shopkeepers and moneymakers, than train-ing us up by bodily drill to the highest of all virtues - the virtue of courage, which is such a very high virtue that with the Greeks the word for it is "manhood".'*

When William Smith, himself a volunteer soldier, was formulating the object of the Boys' Brigade some twenty two years later, we should not be surprised to see that he espoused a 'True Christian Manliness'.

Unfortunately, forty years later, the supposed location of the Junior Corps had become confused by some, notably *'her affectionate nephew Sir Tollemache Sinclar Bart.'* (Q) since it is erroneously stated as 'Leith' on the gothic monument (inscribed in 1901). All the contemporary evidence wholly supports the location as being 'Water of Leith' rather than Leith itself. The name 'Water of Leith' was

An ironic juxtaposition
The remains of Catherine Sinclair's Fountain stand in the 'Stedfastgate' Water of Leith Walkway, named in 1983 to celebrate 100 years of The Boys' Brigade.

certainly not in current use in 1901, the area being better known as the 'Dean Village'. Water of Leith however, is where Catherine herself, in a letter to John Hope in November 1861, proudly reports the location to be:

'I know you have taken a friendly interest in my Juvenile Volunteers and wish much if you could spare time to come tomorrow (Saturday) at 3 o'clock to my mission home at the Water of Leith where they are to drill in uniform for the first time.'

Catherine's house in George Street and St John's Church - photo's taken in 2008

Whilst Catherine, a staunch anti-catholic and pro-temperance campaigner herself, was quite willing to take the lead from the fervent abstainer and vitrioloc anti-papist John Hope in regard to how she would operate some aspects of her Juvenile Volunteers, she did not find it necessary to make the young people take a pledge of abstinence. The substantial financial beneficence Catherine brought to the volunteers meant that 'her' cadets would be the first in Edinburgh to wear a uniform.

Catherine seems to have operated in a well-defined area around the West End of Princes' St. where she worshipped at St. John's Episcopal Church. Her home was in George Street and the school premises used by the Volunteers were in nearby Young Street. The Corps/Brigade would certainly have been given basic religious instruction since it was her Christian faith which led Catherine to indulge in the high level of philanthropy that undoubtedly con tributed to her premature death, in August 1864, through 'over-work'. She died at the Kensington vicarage where her brother John, Archdeacon of Middlesex, resided.[150] Her pioneering activity in developing philanthropic works within the City of Edinburgh was continued after her death by another mighty lady, the Baroness Angela Burdett-Coutts, who also provided drinking fountains and was given the freedom of the city in 1874.

John Hope and the 'British League Cadets'

Like his Edinburgh contemporary, Catherine Sinclair, John Hope came from a family distinguished in the areas of military, academia and the law. Born in 1807 he studied law before becoming involved in politics. By 1844 he described himself as *'a young convert'* evidently having become quite religious. Hope was also strongly opposed to the consumption of tobacco and alcohol and against all forms of gambling. In similar vein he was an active campaigner for Sunday observance and active in numerous charitable organisations. Finally, Hope was virulently anti-Catholic and a fervent supporter of the 'No Popery' movement from the 1850s onwards. [151]

British League Bible Class 1866

On 25th February 1846 a conference of Edinburgh Sunday School teachers was held, out of which was born the children's temperance movement. John Hope, who wanted Edinburgh to become a model for that movement, became part of the inaugurating committee. In November of the same year a magazine entitled 'The British League' appeared that adopted a strong temperance and anti-tobacco stance. Hope ordered 5,000 copies and began organising temperance meetings for children. On January 1st 1847 The British League of Juvenile Abstainers was founded and the Edinburgh Branch was the first to be established.

It is important to see John Hope in the context of those who were working for young people in Scotland in the middle decades of the nineteenth century. The Rev. Dr. Thomas Guthrie was, like Hope, a total abstainer who welcomed Hope on the management Committee of his Ragged Industrial School. However, Hope was always more extreme than Guthrie in his anti-Catholic views and his fervent abstinence. In a forthright letter to Guthrie on 13th January 1855 he referred to the alternative Ragged School organisation, founded by Guthrie, as the *'Popish Ragged School'*. Also, Guthrie's support of the Free Church of Scotland did not endear him to Hope who was a staunch Church of Scotland man. Catherine Sinclair, however, as a staunch anti-Catholic and temperance campaigner always got his full support, even when she was campaigning for her fountain *'for animals and humans'*.[152]

Hope's connections were widespread, even if it was often simply as a source of revenue! Lord Elcho, who was eventually to become pre-eminent in encouraging the Volunteer Movement, was, in the early years of Hope's British League, one of his prime targets for funding, as was the Duke of Argyll.[153] It was then, as it sometimes can be today, often a matter of 'who you know' - Lord Elcho's nomination for election as MP was seconded by John Sinclair, Catherine Sinclair's Father.[154]

Officers and NCOs No 16 Company Edinburgh Rifle Volunteers 1866

In 1859, when the Volunteer Movement was launched, Hope was keen to establish an 'abstainers' company. He eventually formed one that became both popular and efficient. The normal motto on the cap badge was *'In Defence not Defiance.'* Hope replaced this with *'God is our Defence'*. It was the young people who Hope saw as his real challenge. His attitude to them was to adopt a mix of discipline and kindness. In a pamphlet detailing the arrangements for the British League excursion in 1859 to Smithy Park, [155] clearly he was aware that the 'handling' of the large numbers involved required military precision. It was stated that on arrival, *'...the children will be formed in close order.'* Then it proceeds:

'Mr Hope requests that no physical force be employed, but that the law of kindness be used, and no other, in keeping order… We would especially warn boys against swinging on or breaking the branches of trees, or entering any plantations.'

With the success of the Volunteer Company, the idea of applying Volunteer methods to the youngsters of the British League of Juvenile Abstainers began to develop in Hope's mind. In preparation for the excursion to Dirleton in July 1860 the superintendents of the young people's meetings were asked to have the apprentices drilled. At the Dirleton meeting itself the young people were asked if they would attend drill classes if these were formed. No less than 139 gave in their names and when it was also announced the drill lessons for the rest would continue 1500 cheers arose. *'It appeared …'*, said Hope to the Right Hon. R. C. Nisbet Hamilton, *'… as if the cheers from the 1500 had awakened an immense rookery.'* [156] Drill was clearly popular. Hope, wasting no time, went about the first act of establishing his Cadets namely the hiring of five drill sergeants - one for each of the five prospective companies. Hope's target group was to be young men already in respectable employment. As he explained in a letter to John Wilson [157] written in July 1860, *'… the object is to …confine it to those who are actually at trades… .'* Later in the same month whilst writing to the Governors of James Gillespie's Hospital [158] to ask for permission to drill 'apprentices' on the grass in front of the hospital he assured them that:

'The patriotic object of the drilling is set forth in the handbill, but I am also very anxious to take advantage of the present interest in favour of drilling, so that these young men may be set up in their future, for I am convinced such drillings and the extension motions, and such employment of their evenings, few of them get to the country, will be productive of much good to their figures and health.'

The Cadets were drilled, in their various companies including the 'No 1' or Grenadier Company made up of the bigger lads who would then transfer into the No 16 Edinburgh Volunteer Company. Hope was aware that in Glasgow a similar Cadet Corps had been established under the auspices of the Southern Volunteer Rifles at South Side Parks. On 28th July 1860, keen to avail himself of the 'know how' in regard to such matters as uniforms, he wrote to the commanding officer, Lt William Cochrane 3rd Lanark V.R., for details. These duly arrived by 30th August.[159] In addition, one suspects, that if he saw it, Hope was pleased to read the following extract from the Glasgow Herald reprinted in the Edinburgh Evening Courant of 7th September 1860:

'Cadet Corps in Glasgow growing with now 70 on the roll. Drilling on Wed. 5th September 1860. Most of the number present were in uniform (consisting of grey blouse and smart hat, with scarlet band) and it is expected that the whole company will be equipped in about a week...the whole appearance of this "Petit Corps" seemed to give great satisfaction to the spectators, of whom a considerable number were present.'

Light, short carbines were ordered for use in drilling and obtained, with the help of the Lord Provost, 225 in total, *' ... at a moderate price.'* [160] Hope insisted that all those who had immediate influence over the boys were not only abstainers from alcohol and tobacco, but also favourable to religion. In January 1861 he took up the references from both the Church and employer of a certain James Sutherland who had applied for the job as Bandmaster for the juveniles. The employer, the Procurator Fiscal at Dornoch, replied: [161] *'Takes odd glass of ale, but doesn't enter a public house. Perfect discipline-goes to church and obedient to all my orders.'* One wonders if the 'odd glass' excluded this particular applicant.

In January 1860 Hope is recorded as writing: *'We propose at last to have a band-a large flute band-in connection with the League, to march in front of our own company when it goes to drill.'* [162] Estimates were obtained for equipping a brass band and a flute band, but it was decided to proceed with the flute band first. A bandmaster was engaged from Glasgow.

Early in 1861 leaflets were distributed at children's meetings seeking recruits for the Cadet Company and the Drum and Flute Band. Hope made it clear that no uniforms would be issued until boys had proved that they were punctual abstainers, well behaved and thoroughly drilled. The British League excursion in 1861 was a much more regimented affair than before with Bugle calls being sounded and the youngsters formed into companies with cadet help. The band was involved in leading the procession. Generally Hope expected to get his own way, and usually got it. However there was opposition. He wrote to William Miller of the Lancastrian School, 4 Hope Park, to request the use of the school for drill. He was firmly rebuffed: [163]

'The Volunteer movement, though undertaken by some, I believe, from what they consider patriotic motives, I cannot but regard as highly injurious to the moral feelings of the young men who engage in it and, therefore, I should feel myself highly blameworthy were I in any way to encourage it. The tendency is to destroy the sense of the inviolability of human life by accustoming them to look upon dexterity in the destruction of those whom they call their country's enemies as a worthy attainment, not considering that these are alike objects of Divine regard with themselves, and equally with them of the number of those for whom Christ died.'

Although some were evidently appalled by Hope's endeavours others, such as Catherine Sinclair were, quick to make use of his experience. In a letter sent during April 1861 [164] she wrote:

'I have asked Mr Sandford to call upon you tomorrow that we may obtain your advice in the arrangement of an evening class for boys which I wish to establish entirely at my own cost. No man is more experienced than you in every good work on behalf of the young. I should like to obtain your recommendation of a master and suggestion what salary to give him.'

Interestingly, in his reply Hope reveals that where the British League was operating at the Water of Leith, there existed some conflict of interest. For, on Thursday evenings, between 6 and 7 o'clock, boys who should have been attending the British League abstinence meeting were opting instead to take part in drill at Catherine Sinclair's school hall. Hope complained that, *'...we only had a few girls.'*

The Scotsman newspaper reported the General Meeting of George Heriot's Hospital in 1861 along with a detailed submission from Hope as to the progress of his work. He was careful to itemise only those aspects of his Cadet training which he knew would be accepted by everyone, viz. the *'pleasing recreation'* and the *'national importance'*. Clearly he didn't wish to alienate the management of Heriot's Hospital with which he had undertaken correspondence three years previously regarding the serving of wine to its boys on Founder's Day.

'The result of the summer work has been to produce a large company of apprentices thoroughly drilled; in company and battalion drill, and I fully expect in spring to turn

out 200 well-drilled cadets with carbines, headed by a juvenile drum and flute band of from fifty to sixty boys, all up to their respective duties, and I cannot but think this exercise will prove very beneficial to the health of the boys, and a pleasing recreation, and suitable occupation to them on some evenings of the week after their day's work is over; and in addition to these considerations, we know that the drilling of the young is viewed in the highest quarters as of great importance in a national point of view. In further evidence of the importance of juvenile drill I subjoin the following letter which I received from Lieutenant Colonel Davidson, E.R.V. :-

Woodcroft, 1st August 1861.
'Dear Sir - I shall be glad to hear that you have got accommodation in the Corn Exchange for the drill of your cadets. I attach the utmost importance to the extension of the Volunteer movement to the rising generation, who, if the thing lasts, will form the staple of our citizen soldiers a few years hence. I wish Government would give decided encouragement to it in all our large schools, giving them drill, gratis.' [165]

By 1861 there were 240 'effective members' of the cadets, drilling 'late and early' in schoolrooms and yards throughout the city. The cadets were not short on numbers, but standards were high and evidently the 'turnover' was quite high too, especially within the Band. There is correspondence from Hope to the Police with regards to boys from the British League Band who having enjoyed a 'strawberry feast' at his house were set upon by boys who were formerly members of the Band. Apparently these had formed themselves into another separate unit - the Midlothian Band.[166]

In November 1860 Hope had written to A. K. Murray of 7th Lanarkshire Rifles after reading letters from him about his Glasgow Juvenile Corps published in The Scotsman.[167] Murray eventually sent samples which were returned on 11th August 1862 by which time the Cadet uniform had been chosen. By March 1862 proto-types had been made. Cadets would wear a red Garibaldi shirt, blue knickerbockers, brown leggings, red Garibaldi forage caps with badge and light brown leather belts with frogs and a clasp bearing the initials 'B.L.C.'. Significantly, given the direction 'Brigade uniform' would take in the future, the chosen 'uniform' was in effect a set of glorified accoutrements. The scarlet shirts were made to go over a boy's jacket. The knickerbockers with scarlet braid were over-trousers bound to the leg by thick canvas leggings edged in leather. In fact, the scarlet cap was the same as the Scots Greys undress cap. Hope's description was, *'...very showy, comfortable and easily fitted in different sizes.'* The cost per uniform was 3s - to 1/6d. There was a 'one size fits all' (or at least as few as two sizes) approach to uniform. Perhaps not the 'showy' aspect, but Hope's whole approach to providing a 'uniform' for his cadets was driven by cost. It was important to him that the expense would not prevent potential members from joining. Just like the Boys' Brigade more than twenty years later, his solution was to provide accoutrements to be worn over normal clothing.

Cadet Officer.

Uniforms of the British League Cadets

On July 5th 1862, the cadets turned-out for the first time in uniform. There were 120 of them including the band on parade in the High School Yards. Mr George Wedderburn, who was present at the inspection that day, wrote to Hope commenting, not on the uniforms but on the general appearance of the boys.[168]

'I never saw a cleaner set of boys and the playing of the band was a good deal beyond what I was prepared for. With regard to the "audience" they had collected in the course of their march I could not see the advantage - useful perhaps to give me an opportunity of contrasting the "raw material". When in Palermo I saw "Garibaldi's Own" and this well drilled also, they had not the neat clean appearance of the League Cadets.' There seems to have been some friction when the uniforms were issued as perhaps they were a bit too garish for some, perhaps attracting spiteful name calling. However, parents were, it appears, generally delighted to see their offspring regaled as part of the cadets. Mr. W. Urquhart, of 32 Arthur Street, wrote to Hope on 28th Sept 1862:

'Sir-I must thank you for your continued kindness to my son Lockhart for clothing him as a Cadet and giving him the best of education and keeping him in the faith of virtue and temperance.'

Over the next few years the Cadet Corps seems to have settled down, the bright red 'Garibaldi' uniforms becoming

The badge of the British League Cadets

commonplace on parades and events. It turned out for Lord Palmerston's visit in 1863, and for many distinguished guests of the Lord Provost. For instance, the 1868 Review of Volunteers in the Queen's Park featured 235 members of the Cadet Corps. By 1868, there was also a Cadet Brass Band. In 1883, the year of foundation of The Boys' Brigade, John Hope's Cadets at their annual inspection mustered a healthy 195 plus the band.

Cadets could earn prizes for attendance at drill. One popular prize was at Hope's own expense. This involved awarding a pair of stout boots each year to every qualifying cadet. For the older Grenadiers it was also possible to be rewarded with a pair of trousers or some other clothing. This scheme operated for a period of some twenty-two years, during which time 2064 pairs of boots, or nearly 100 pairs a year, were distributed among the boys. Further encouragement was given by awarding free invitations to the annual British League

**Mr George McGibbon
('Mr Hope's right-hand man')
and the British League Office
at 53 Rose St.**

excursion. A medal for 'veterans', with attendance at 50 drills, had been instituted in 1862.

The status quo, however, was not to be maintained. In the late 1880s, the quasi-independent 'Abstainers Company' of Volunteers seems to have been questioned and the British League Cadets was advised to become attached to a 'regular' E.R.V. corps. Members of the 'Abstainers Company' joined a new 3rd Edinburgh Rifle Volunteer Company and the British League Cadets became attached to it. Perhaps by way of compensation Hope was awarded the title 'Hon. Captain of the British League Cadets'. On January 2nd 1891 The Edinburgh Evening News reported on a British League Soiree:

'...under the auspices of the BL was held last night in the Literary Institute. Major David Campbell, who presided, said the League was instituted so long ago as 1st January 1847 and that it was as strong today as ever. He was able to say that the League was not only to be found in Edinburgh, but also in many parts of the world. He claimed that the establishment of the Boys' Brigade was suggested by the starting of the British League Corps by Col. Hope...'

The Cadets seem to have continued until 1892 [169] when they disappeared from the Army List. John Hope died on Sunday 25th June 1893, and his funeral was held in Greyfriars on the following Wednesday. The Hope Trust, created in 1890 to perpetuate his life's work, remains active, funding a variety of religious, educational and temperance programmes. A letter to The Edinburgh Evening News of 1st July 1937, answering one in an earlier edition which claimed survivors of the 1881 Volunteer Review had then to be of a great age, questioned that assumption. Hugh Pringle, then aged 67, stated that as a boy of 11, he had attended the review as a member of John Hope's Cadet flute band. According to Pringle the Cadets were known as the 'Water Rats'.

John Hope's British League Cadets was, certainly for the first twenty years, clearly not a 'normal' cadet corps, albeit a pioneer organisation. The founder wanted to find some way to control the boys attending temperance classes and provide a worthy recreation for their spare time. To do this he drew upon his Volunteer experience.

The name 'cadets' was used rather than 'brigade', perhaps to distinguish the members from the shoe-blacks and similar recipients of charity and to emphasise the 'military' aspects - the very term 'brigade' was not then associated with the 'military' as it may be today. It was a child of the Sunday school movement and from the outset the programme included instruction in temperance and Christianity. It could be said that the 'twin pillars' of the organisation were religion and discipline. Members were 'working class' boys, apprentices who lived at home and, given the levels of commitment required, must have, in the main, received substantial encouragement from their parents to become members, in the same way as did Boys' Brigade members.

CHAPTER SEVEN

Temperance and Teetotal

The influence of intoxicating liquor upon the masses of people within large industrial towns and cities in the 19th century is well documented. Working class young people, as well as those living on the streets, faced, and quite frequently yielded to, the daily temptations of alcohol. In looking for the origins of the brigade movement we can discern quite clearly that one of its roots is the early temperance and abstinence juvenile institutions or societies set up with the prime aim of combating the demon drink.

The motivation of the early pioneers in what we would today call 'youth work' was generally a mixture of Christian religious doctrine and social reformation, with the one supporting and justifying the other. For some, the priority was a matter of providing food, physical education and the three 'R's', whilst for others it was making possible the ascent of the first step on the ladder of employment. Christian, particularly Protestant Christian teaching, was the dominant force for many, particularly in Scotland, whilst for others training the nation's future soldiers and sailors seemed a worthy aim in itself. Widespread use and abuse of intoxicating alcoholic drink was seen by many as one of the greatest barriers preventing social elevation and reform, making education, employment and religious conversion almost impossible. For these reasons Abstinence and Temperance were both themes widely taken up by those wishing to extend the kingdom of Christ and further their particular personal aspect of social reform. Dr. Thomas Chalmers was a major supporter of Temperance: *'Let me record my sense of the value of temperance and my friendliness to temperance societies.'* [170] The methods adopted by those working with young people to oppose the influences of drink, from the late 18th century and into and throughout the 19th century, provide a pattern, much of which was taken-up by the Boys' Brigade and its imitators.

A notable example of the way in which one Sunday school teacher, Volunteer, anti-papist and total abstainer, employed brigade methods to further his cause can be found in chapter six concerning John Hope and his British League Cadets in 1840s Edinburgh. The Temperance movement in Scotland was more than ten years old by 1840 following on from the reduction in the tax on spirits in 1822. According to Elspeth King, [171] drinking to capacity was seen as a national characteristic, if not a virtue in 18th century Scotland. It was John Dunlop (1789-1868) a Greenock lawyer and philanthropist who became recognised in his own lifetime as *'the father of Temperance in Great Britain'*. He established temperance societies in Maryhill and Greenock early in October 1829. Dunlop attracted the support of William Collins the printer and publisher who was an admirer and disciple of Dr Thomas Chalmers and an elder in the Tron Church, Glasgow when Chalmers was Minister: '...*Dunlop was the moving spirit behind and prime organiser of the first general temperance movement in Britain.*' [172] The Glasgow City Mission, founded in 1826, provided strong support for Temperance, and cotton manufacturer Robert Kettle (1761-1852), one of its first subscribers, became President of the Glasgow Abstinence Society and later President of the Scottish Temperance League founded in 1844. [173]

A significant step forward in promoting temperance to young people came in October 1832 with the formation, by Dunlop of *'The Greenock Youth's Society for the Promotion of Temperance'*.[174] Members signed an *'Engagement'* (which became known as 'The Pledge'.) Abstainers and Temperance worked together, there being 390 members by 1833. In 1834, the town was divided into districts (on the lines suggested by Chalmers) and 44 visitors were appointed to promote it among the young, to give out tracts and to organise visitations and meetings. By 1833, of the 400 Temperance Societies in Scotland 93 were for youths which had a membership of 5,841.[175] In 1835, there was a split between the Abstainers and the Temperance with abstainers such as Edward Morris in Glasgow taking the lead and forming new societies. In his book, published in 1855, Morris reported on the Annual Meeting of the Abstainers' Union in 1842 when the formation of juvenile societies was not only noted, but seen as vital work.[176] Morris further extolled the *'great exertions'* which were made, from 1847 - 1850, to organise Youths' Temperance Associations such as the Anderston Young People's Juvenile Society of Teetotallers in the 1850s. Juvenile societies were also formed in Hamilton, Greenock, Camlachie and Parkhead, with the largest society in the Gorbals having 750 members: '...*a special effort to enlist the young on the side of abstinence'*. [177] For the Queen's Birthday, 19th May 1849, 650 members of Glasgow, Cowcaddens, Anderston and Partick Juvenile Societies walked in procession to the Botanic Gardens, '... *adorned with medals, rosettes, ribbons etc. and accompanied by flags and banners.'* [178] On the 10th Sept. 1849 there was a Juvenile Abstinence Demonstration in the City Hall where an address was made to the Prince of Wales. Morris stated that, *'They marched, many of them with their little peaceful banners, to the place of meeting.'* There were some 4,000 present, aged from 6 -16 years, '... *many of them decorated with ribbons, sashes, temperance medals, etc..'* [179 & 180] There were 6,870 juvenile members in the Glasgow Association. The Scottish Temperance League, based in Hope Street, Glasgow, issued a torrent of literature, song books, novels and tracts and an illustrated monthly publication for children called *'The Adviser'*. The language used to publicize Juvenile Temperance societies reveals that, even as early as 1849, a military tone and analogy was quite acceptable. In an article entitled, *'Ought Parents to Encourage their Children to Become Members of Juvenile Abstinence Societies?'* the following phrases appear: *'not only armed within, but armed without.'*, *'with his armour on.'*, *'And this is his shield...'* and *'the battle is fought and won.'* [181] The 1850 Review emphasised the importance of training: *'Our juvenile societies are indeed numerous and constantly increasing...our bands must be trained bands. Our armies must be disciplined armies. We must, by all means, secure for them the very best training and discipline that are to be had...otherwise our hosts will faint, or flee, on the day of battle...'* Training included: no drink, instruction in the cause and its history, and a temperance catechism.[182] A great gathering of 20,000 Juvenile Abstainers was held in Edinburgh on 5th July 1851, some 12,000 were from Edinburgh and 6,000 from Glasgow. They were reported as being, *'... generally clean and many of them neatly dressed.'* [183]

The Band of Hope

This was a non-denominational juvenile temperance organisation, catering for all children up to 16 years which began in Leeds in 1847 and became for more than half a century one of the most widely supported youth movements in Britain. Its ideology was the rearing of children in sobriety rather than trying to reclaim their parents. Individual Bands were given their own autonomy to operate exciting programmes of free lantern lectures, soirees and excursions. The Scottish Band of Hope Union was founded in Glasgow in 1871 in order to co-ordinate the efforts of many different organisations which had come into being. The first Chairman was William Quarrier, the founder of the Glasgow Shoe-black Brigade, the City Orphanage and the Orphan Homes of Scotland, Bridge of Weir. In a speech at the Temperance Congress of 1862 in London, Thomas Bowick from Kenilworth expected the Band of Hope to be doing what, some 21 years later the Boys' Brigade was doing: *'We should never expect to find properly trained Band of Hope children, or senior youths, frequenting "the idle corner" Which unfortunately, every town and village can boast of.'* [184] In many ways Bowick intuitively knew what seemed to be the correct course of action. He witnessed the youngsters meeting together for good and useful training: *'Young people love to be associated together; and if associated in a good cause, the one strengthens the good resolutions of the other...'* [185] The words he was looking for were in fact that credo of the Public School - *'esprit de corps'*. Bowick had clearly needed to defend his position from those who said that banding together young people weakened parental influence, but he called it *'nonsense'*, being quite clear about the alternative which was, *'...the contaminating influence of the street is left to do its work unchecked.'* [186] In 1870, the Band of Hope had 650 Juvenile societies in Scotland. [187] Bands of Hope, and similar juvenile temperance societies were not *'uniformed'* as such, but there was no shortage of militaristic language, style and tone. For the anniversary of The Scottish Temperance League in Glasgow in 1872, it was reported that, *'...the Bands of Hope in the several quarters of the city mustered at different points and marched in procession to the City Hall in three detachments, headed by flute bands.'* [188] In 1884, the Band of Hope Unions in the UK numbered some 735 with a total membership of 111,000. [189] This was probably the largest juvenile organisation in the country until the Boys' Brigade was formed. Interestingly, Walter Mallock Gee, who founded the Church Lads' Brigade, in 1891, had written, just a few months before, what was to become a famous practical text book for Band of Hope workers, *'The Nation's Hope'*. He was in 1890, full-time Secretary of the Junior Division of the Church of England Temperance Society. In Gee's book The Boys' Brigade is recommended and an entire chapter devoted to it. [190] Gee was always proud of the fact that the first CLB Branch of the Junior Church of England Temperance Society was established in his own No 1. St Andrew's - the Pioneer Company. Some early Boys' Brigade companies were formed in connection with the Band of Hope movement such as the 1st Witney Coy in Oxfordshire, formed by the Wesleyan Methodist Band of Hope.[191] In 1906, recognising the problem of teenage rebellion, the Crusader movement was formed to accommodate those too old for the Band and too young for adult temperance societies.

Adult Temperance Societies with Juvenile Branches

Virtually all of the adult temperance societies found that it was essential to establish a juvenile organisation or section, often within the first decade of their existence.

The Independent Order of Rechabites, grew out of the Total Abstinence movement and the Temperance Burial Society in Manchester and Salford in 1835. Modelled on the typical Friendly Societies such as the Oddfellows, Foresters, Druids, Shepherds and Buffaloes regalia, ritual and passwords were adopted from the outset. Rechabites were divided into Districts, but organised in Tents like the ancient Israelites from whence the name came. The society was introduced into Scotland by John Macintosh, the Guard on the Edinburgh to Liverpool stagecoach who, in 1838, set up the first Tent in Dumfries. The 2nd

Tent was formed in Edinburgh the same year, with Glasgow, Greenock and Port Glasgow all established by 1839. [192] By 1841 there were 523 Tents in the UK of which 47 were in Scotland with some 4,000 members, many of whom would have been juveniles, particularly in the west of Scotland where juvenile tents were described as being, '...*of vast importance*.' [193] The avant-garde of the tee-total movement, the Rechabites, was allowed to head the great west of Scotland procession to Glasgow Green in July 1841: '...*the Rechabite division of the teetotal army...in full dress, with the insignia of their Order, led the van, and from their uniform and respectable appearance, bespoke a favourable feeling for those who followed*.' [194] Juvenile Rules and Instruction cards were issued for the first time between 1841-2, some 2,000 being sold. A Juvenile Tent with 40 members, was opened in Greenock on 15th October 1841 which was known as '*The Pride of Greenock*'. [195] In January 1841 a procession in Alloa was reported:

'*The officers and brethren wore their sashes and led the van, followed by the Phoenix Hope Juvenile Tent...and in this manner they marched to Clackmannan to meet...the Tower Hill Tent ...all wearing emblems of the Order and each with a white wand, preceded by two pipers assisted by two drummers, the procession returned into the town...*'

During 1841-42 the Juvenile ritual was settled and by 1863 it was recorded that, '...*the state of the Juvenile Order is encouraging*.' Nevertheless, the establishment of more tents was still being promoted. [196] A practical way of assisting Juvenile work was sanctioned in 1877 with a '*penny levy*' being imposed to raise funds. [197] In the 1870s there was a great resurgence of interest in the movement. In the Rechabite and Temperance Magazine of 1874 a major article entitled '*The Importance of Forming Juvenile Rechabite Tents*' stated that:

'*It is very important...to instil right principles into the mind of our youth, and lead them to cultivate habits of industry, economy and forethought. A great mistake is made when the young are overlooked, and the whole situation bestowed upon adults.*'

Clearly, not all of the '*senior*' Rechabites were giving the juveniles the attention they deserved. The article argued that the Juvenile Tent must be: '...*a place of healthy discipline - and a kind of training school in which the members are fitted for future operations*.' [198] At the time of Jubilee in 1885, just two years after the formation of The Boys' Brigade, there were some 16,916 juveniles nationally, the sort of numbers not reached by the BB until 1890. Glasgow alone had 949 Juveniles in membership. New Juvenile emblems, music and rituals were start

EDINBURGH CASTLE.

" The children of the drinker will be unstable and untrustworthy, and cannot be expected to walk straight, either in body or mind."—*Plato.*

Modern Science confirms the ancient philosopher. Become a total abstainer and join the Sons of Temperance.

Issued by The Order of the Sons of Temperance Friendly Society
Membership, 300,000   Funds, £675,000.

ed and the benefits of creating the *'nurseries of the Order'* in the 1870s were reaping benefits with a huge growth in numbers. The first National Juvenile Conference was held at the Temperance Hall in Temple Street Birmingham on the 12th April 1887. Numbers continued to increase over the following decade and when the Juvenile Rechabite Magazine began in 1890 it had a circulation of 32, 000 per month. By 1910, Juvenile Rechabite membership in the UK had reached a staggering 189,153 nearly twice the size of the maximum UK BB membership - achieved in 1934.[199]

The Order of the Sons of Temperance started in New York in 1842 was a great success on that side of the Atlantic. The first divisions in the UK were opened in London in 1847 and by 1866 there were so many branches in Scotland that a *'Grand Division'* was started. The usual Friendly Society tradition of rituals and regalia was instituted, the emblem being a star of temperance within a triangle of love, purity and fidelity using the colours red, white and blue. Originally the badge had been white, but this had been replaced about 1900 due to it becoming easily soiled. The Church Lads' Brigade, founded by a Band of Hope enthusiast, also adopted a white *'for purity'* buttonhole badge in the 1890s for its members who had signed the pledge. The female branch of the S.O.T. was usually known as the *'Daughters of Temperance'*. It was the juvenile branch, however, which became outstandingly popular, introducing children to principles of thrift with a variety of educational activities linked with all the spice of belonging to a secret society. That society was called *'Cadets of Temperance'*. When the first sections were formed in Liverpool in 1850, the choice of the militaristic term *'Cadets'* was quite deliberate: members were in training to join an army fighting against the evils of drink. In 1860, Bro. Joseph Thomas reported, *'A very important auxiliary to our Order are the Cadets of Temperance; nevertheless, there is very little attention given to them…in course of time the boys will build up your Divisions.'* [200] By 1867 there were 21 Cadet Sections which had grown to 379 by 1897. In 1882, special Cadet Rules and offices were established to cope with the growing number of members which rose from 2,173 that year to 17,116 by 1897.[201]

At the Grove Street mission - the very epicentre of Glasgow abstinence - the *'Band of Hope'* for young people, was a vital part of the work which commenced immediately upon the opening of the new premises in 1866. From the start, in addition to the military nomenclature, the activities used simple accoutrements worn over normal clothing, along with banners and bands to instil the idea of *'esprit de corps'* amongst the youngsters, all under 15 years of age. J. Wakefield MacGill expounded the achievements of the mission in his speech reported in Ragged School Work in 1886:

'When we got into our commodious premises, we started one of the most successful Bands of Hope I have ever been connected with. Few places had the advantage which we possessed in accommodation. The large hall held about 1,200 children. The organisation was divided into departments. (1) The Cadets of Temperance. These were boys from 11 to 15 years of age. Each lad had a handsome red scarf, with the emblem of his society on it. They had a red and gold banner, of which they were very proud. Their banner bearer took his place each night on the left-hand side of the chairman. (2) We had the Junior Daughters of Temperance, from 11 - 15, with green scarfs. They had a white and gold banner, and their banner bearer took her place on the right-hand side of the chairman. (3) We had the infants' school formed into the Buds of promise. They had a green and gold banner, and their banner bearer also occupied a place on the platform.'

All the children in the Ragged school were involved in the Band of Hope meetings, each class having its own banner: boys-red and girls-green. The most regular attenders, with the best behaviour, carried the banner on Band of Hope night. *'These banner bearers marched round the hall, and when the new members were enrolled, formed a semicircle on the platform. We had the use of a drum and fife band, and sometimes a brass band.'* [202]

The Independent Order of Good Templars was formed in the USA in 1852 and arrived in Scotland when the first Lodge was instituted on 13th August

1869 in Glasgow by Thomas Roberts an exiled Scot. Although not a Friendly Society, like the Rechabites, it used regalia and ritual nevertheless and injected much new life into the abstinence movement which had been losing its momentum. Boosted by the visits of Moody and Sankey in 1874, equal membership rights for men and women, extensive provision for juvenile lodges and educational work, the *'Grand Lodge of Scotland'* was formed and the movement spread like wildfire. By 1893 there were some eighty adult lodges and thirty Juvenile lodges in Glasgow alone, and a total of 70,000 members throughout Scotland. The Good Templars wished to prohibit the manufacture, importation and sale of all intoxicating liquors used as a beverage. The Order was also very patriotic. In 1897, a march to Bannockburn with flags, banners and ten bands was organised to protest against drink which was regarded as the real national enemy. There was also an international outlook with the *'International Good Templar'* quarterly magazine being edited and published in Glasgow. Scotland had the largest lodges in the world, ranging from 25 in Thurso, to 4,198 in Airdrie.

Although the Boys' Brigade originated very near the centre of Glasgow abstinence, it did not actively promote it in the weekly programme. Other groups, such as the Bands of Hope were encouraged to work alongside the Brigade, but not directly through it. William Smith did not encourage pledge-taking by boys. According to Springhall, *'Some companies were, however, to be formed by abstinence societies, for example in Wick and Port Glasgow'.* [203] On the other hand, The Church Lads' Brigade, formed by the ex-secretary of the Junior Branch of the Church of England Temperance Society, in its early years, very much encouraged pledge-taking and company affiliation to the national society was encouraged. [R]

Many of the *'uniformed'*, juvenile temperance organisations and sections continued well into the 20th century. The militaristic tone which had featured in the growth of these organisations, remained prominent right up to the First World War. It was the temperance marching bands which outlived other sections insofar as uniform was concerned.

Early 20th Century Boys' Temperance Bands.
Note the similarity to BB 'accoutrement' uniform

CHAPTER EIGHT

Young Men's Christian Association

George Williams
Founder of the YMCA

The YMCA, particularly in Glasgow, is part of the Brigade story, not just because William Smith was a member from 1872, but because it was an organisation aimed at the *'Intellectual, Moral and Religious Improvement of the Young Men of Glasgow'*.[204] For many years before the start of the Boys' Brigade, the YMCA and similar organisations tried to come to terms with the thirteen to seventeen year olds, particularly as they saw these youngsters as future recruits to their ranks. It had been young men themselves who had brought the YMCA into existence, fuelled with a spirit and vitality that was born with the Evangelical Union, the same dynamism which eventually led to the Disruption in the Church of Scotland.

The usual date given for the founding of the YMCA, 6th June, 1844, is when the organisation was formed in London. However, as Clyde Binfield states:

'By the 1840s Scotland already had a widespread, loosely organized young men's movement, fuelled by Scottish Congregationalists and fuelling the present Scottish YMCA Glasgow, the earliest, was founded in 1824; Paisley in 1832.' [205].

The originator of the Scottish movement was David Naismith who as well as starting the *'Glasgow Young Men's Society for Religious Improvement'* for 14 - 35 year olds in 1824, founded many similar Young Men's Societies as he travelled widely around the UK and North America. His lasting monument is the

London City Mission. Unfortunately, burning himself out by the time he was forty, he died in 1839. The Glasgow Young Men's Society for Religious Improvement became known as the *'Glasgow Young Men's Christian Institute'* in 1841. The last word was replaced with *'Association'* in 1848 after a visit from George Williams in 1844.[206] The *'Glasgow Young Men's Union'* was formed in the city after the visit by evangelist D. L. Moody in 1873.[207] By 1877 the two Glasgow groups had united into the *'Glasgow United YMCA.'* The new Association ran a Library, Literary Institute, had an Annual sermon, Evening classes and Reading Societies. After the amalgamation in 1877, the YMCA - with the Scottish Sunday School Union and the Glasgow Foundry Boys Religious Society - moved into the new Christian Institute, which was being opened in Bothwell Street, in 1878.[208]

George Williams, who was still a draper's apprentice in Somerset when Naismith died, was, *'...in every way a more credible person'* [209] than Naismith. The three major determinants of his life were Drapery, Evangelicalism, and Temperance.[210] Williams moved to London in 1841 to take up a post in Hitchcock's a large department store with an expanding drapery department, eventually becoming a partner and, by 1863, sole proprietor. Personal encounter and small praying groups were central to his religious life. He organised prayer and discussion meetings whilst working with three of the Capital's Congregational Chapels: the King's Weigh House's Domestic Mission and Sunday school, the Surrey Chapel's Ragged School (south of the river) and Craven Chapel's in the West End. Williams, who became an Anglican in the 1850s, was in a very influential position. When he became Churchwarden of Portman Chapel Williams worshipped alongside such people as Lord Shaftesbury. Shaftesbury would later become the president of the London YMCA whilst Williams was treasurer. The relationship between the two men eventually became quite close. Williams succeeded Shaftesbury as President in 1886 after the death of his friend. His Christian development was further inspired by the American revivalists Calvin Colton and G.C. Finney (1859) and later by D. L. Moody (from 1873).

The YMCA had been set up by a dozen young men in a room at 72 St Paul's Churchyard in 1844 and Williams was acknowledged to be its founder. The YMCA succeeded and grew rapidly because of the methods used by Williams: *'George Williams....had the draper's sixth sense; a rapid ability to sum up and clothe his fellow men, appropriate to their station'.*[211] He stated: *'Get to know the names of young men. Take one at a time. Write a letter to him, give him a shake of the hand, ask him to have a friendly cup of tea; talk kindly, naturally with him; take him for a walk; show him a little kindness, and you will get hold of him.'* [212] It is hardly surprising that William Smith was drawn towards this movement. In 1894, Williams was knighted and the YMCA had 150,000 members in Britain, 450,000 in the USA, and 120,000 in Germany amongst many others. At the time of his death, in 1905, he was said to be president of 39 societies including the United Kingdom Band of Hope.

Between 1861 and 1870 some twenty-two Associations were established in Scotland and were seen to be leading the way in working with young people. Dundee, in 1864, was typical, having 570 members and owning its own building. Here there was a reading room, reference library, parlour and gymnasium. Bible Classes, prayer and praise meetings, boys' and girls' services, evangelical services and temperance meetings were regular features along with education in science and the arts. The main problem was seen as, *'...sustaining the interest of the younger members.'* [213] The YMCA's triangular emblem, denoting fitness of body, mind and spirit represented the cutting-edge holistic approach of the Association. The Annual Reports of the Scottish National Council of YMCAs demonstrate a rapid growth with an increasing focus upon work with boys and girls. In 1878, there were 123 Associations with a total membership of 15,195, with some 4,872 in Glasgow alone. Aberdeen and Gourock had boys' meetings, Bathgate ran a 'Children's Church', Hamilton operated a Saturday night boys and girls meeting and Tillicoutry laid on special children's services. [214] By 1879, *'classes for neglected boys and girls'* were being run in Montrose whilst in Aberdeen a *'Boys' meeting was held, which had proved a great success.'*. In Glasgow it seemed that large numbers of the young preferred YMCA classes to those of the School Board. A military flavour was appearing in some of the language adopted, perhaps seen as quite relevant by the young men to whom it was addressed. For instance, a discussion on the *'Aggressive Work of the YMCA'* was reported, describing the young men's training in Prayer meetings, Fellowships and Evangelistic meetings, *'...to the use of that weapon which will make them effective "Soldiers of the Cross".'* [215] Membership numbers were falling off a little when Mr. Young of Alva made a suggestion, *'The way to make Associations successful in small towns is to form Juvenile Associations...to institute libraries, to start cricket clubs and to provide other means of attracting and amusing the members.'* Other ideas to boost membership were coming from Boston (USA): gym, rambling clubs, bicycle clubs, football clubs, swimming clubs, charity work, an employment exchange and a boarding house. Other 'imported' ideas included Parlour Meetings with piano, tea, talks, hymns, music and 'singing the gospel', providing a restaurant as happened in Manchester, and a Seaside House in North Wales.[216] Boys and children's meetings were reported in 1884 as being held in Crosshill, Alloa, Alva, Clackmannan, Dollar, Sauchie, Falkirk, Stirling, South Queensferry, Dalbeattie and Aberdeen. The Travelling Secretary of the YMCA in Scotland reported:

'How to keep hold of young lads at the age when they drift away from the Sabbath School and often from the Minister's Bible Class, has been successfully solved in several Associations, by dealing with the lads as a class by themselves.'

Here, for the first time in the YMCA someone has put his finger on the nub of the issue. A meeting on 'Boys 12 to 15 years of age' led by Joseph Shepherd, took place in Dundee, but unfortunately there are no other details given.[217] The Travelling Secretary continued to make his point the following year:

'Another source of weakness…is the neglect of the boys and youths…we now believe in gaining the younger lads. This department of work was emphasised at the International Conference, London, 1881, The British Conference Liverpool, 1883 and our National Conference Galashiels in 1884….Our American brethren are devoting much time and expensive effort to its extension in the US. It now forms a separate branch of work in 9 of our Associations…'.[218]

Clearly, there was a good deal of momentum for male youth-work being built-up in the first few years of the 1880s. How easy would this have been for William Smith to ignore? The YMCA would prove to be a great ally in the formation and development of The Boys' Brigade in its earliest days. In 1890, with some 248 Associations and 24,459 members the Association was apparently doing quite well in Scotland. These raw figures, of little help today in understanding how the Association was coping with its junior members, seemed to provide just as much confusion at the time. The Travelling Secretary, whilst proud to announce the Association's formation of Boys' Brigade companies, and emphasising the importance of the work, cannot put any numbers to it:

'A growing interest has been shown for years in junior sections…We cannot, in the regrettable absence of general statistical returns, say with what result. Some

Associations i.e. Brechin, Callander, Dunfermline, etc., have raised successful compa nies of the Boys' Brigade, while others, such as for example, as Dunkeld and Inverness, have formed good youths or junior sections. This department of the work is of great and constant moment.' [219]

Evangelists Moody and Sankey paid further visits during 1892 and boys and children's meetings were reported as well as the Boys' Brigade companies. [220] The Travelling Secretary was no doubt pleased that in 1893 Associations were required to register if they had, *'Junior Members or Associates'* and there were 279 so registered. He was still rather frustrated, it would seem, when he appealed for a change of attitude: *'When will our YMCAs learn that if we are to win the young men we must begin work with the boys?'* A member of each Association should be devoted, *'…to the lads of the place as a branch of the YMCA work.'* [221] With an increase to 799 junior members the following year the report was a little more positive in its outlook: *'Many Associations have begun to realize the importance of undertaking special work on behalf of boys, and as a result, Junior Branches have been formed in many towns and villages.'* [222]

William Smith, who was clearly in tune with the aims, ideals and aspirations of the YMCA, started an organisation more fitted to the evident needs of the boys, with whom he was also on a similar wavelength. The Boys' Brigade, in many places, effectively became the junior branch of the YMCA. Smith was quite happy to see that his boys, upon leaving the Brigade, moved on to become members of the YMCA rather than simply members of the church congregation.

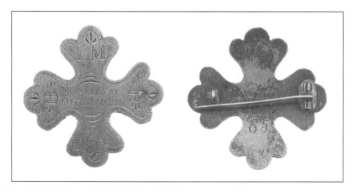

A very early YMCA-BB medal, awarded by Myers & Marble June 13th 1885

CHAPTER NINE

The Free College Church
Glasgow 1877 - 1895

The National Archives of Scotland provide us with Annual Reports for the Free College Church [223] which provided the very cradle, crucible and context into which the Brigade was born, as well as its nursery through the formative years. Here we find the influences upon Mr. W. A. Smith, and his various ideas and experiments as the idea of a Boys' Brigade took shape.

The 1877 report acknowledged that the 1872 Education Act had reduced the need for an Education Fund. The general direction of the social work of the church was evidently changing under the dynamic leadership of the Rev. George Reith D.D.. The Mission at South Woodside was proving to be inadequate and a lease was taken on temporary mission premises at North Woodside. The new mission was expected to be a success since there was a *growing population all around'*. The report also added: *'The Deacons' Court are hopeful…a good and successful work may be done there, in the way of Sabbath Schools, Evening Meetings and other Missionary labours.'* More money, however, was needed. Ministerial classes for Young Men and Young Ladies over fifteen years were operating, as was the Young Men's Society, the Dorcas Society, The Choir, and Sunday Afternoon Children's Classes. Ten Children's classes operated, five for boys and five for girls. William Smith was a member of the Young Men's Society.

Rev. George Reith

By 1878 there were 394 members of the congregation, regarded even at the time as being small in number, but they were wealthy and active. The temporary quarters at 340, North Woodside Road was getting too small, so a new spacious building with, *'…ample accommodation for Sabbath Schools'* was built with just £1,500 remaining to pay. The District Sabbath Schools were now operating and Mr. W. A. Smith was the Secretary, *'…aided by a most zealous and efficient staff.'* There were seventeen female teachers, nine males and 282 scholars (169 girls and 113 boys), an increase of 58 over the previous year. A Band of Hope was started with Mr. J. Archibald Campbell in charge.

The North Woodside Mission

Although membership had increased slightly by 1879, the Young Men's Society and the Dorcas Society were both in abeyance. However, there was good news on the Mission Hall front as the money had been raised and the Large Hall was opened on 23rd March, *'... suitable and comfortable in every respect.'* The whole building was in use by the time the report was submitted in April 1879. A cookery class and library was started and it was hoped that social events would take place there. It was noted that on the Sabbath afternoon, all the available rooms were used for the District Sabbath School, described as, *'Important and growing work.'* In fact, the school now had 310 scholars (184 girls and 126 boys). William A Campbell had replaced Mr. Bary as Superintendent. This was the same year that the 'Woodside Young Men's Club and Institute' was started, which probably accounts for the demise of the former Young Men's Society. The aim of the new Institute was to retain, *'...the interest of young men when they begin to outgrow the interest of the Sabbath School.'* Classes included: Bible, 3R's, History, Shorthand, Political Economy, and Saturday Evening Entertainment (music, readings, lectures). On three nights per week reading and recreation rooms were open and it was hoped to extend this to every evening. The members, it was hoped, would self-govern it. A small entrance fee was charged and the library, if it was to function, was in need of books. The Band of Hope had increased to 100 members.

In 1880 the influence of Mr. W. A. Smith was being felt throughout the increasingly active Mission. He is listed as Secretary of the Woodside Young Men's Club and Institute, now, remarkably, meeting every week-day night at 8.00 p.m.:

'The WYMCI during the past year has had a much more vigorous career than heretofore, and much of this success is due to the energetic secretary, Mr. W. A. Smith'

There were 58 members as against just 17 the year before. The established aims were to, '...assist religious and intellectual self-culture', but also to provide 'innocent social enjoyment.' The reading room, library and recreation room, were now all up and running. On one Saturday each month there were entertainments such as music and reading which made the place, '... crowded to overflowing'. In fact, the new Mission Hall was starting to feel quite cramped with some 448 scholars in the District Sabbath School and a new Temperance Society being formed there.

The Sabbath School membership exceeded five hundred for the first time in 1881, but the WYMCI was down to just 26. A new Debating Society was started as was a Mothers' Meeting and Young Women's Meeting. The real success of 1882 was, again, the Sabbath School and consequently the Mission buildings were, '...taxed to their utmost.' Smith's Sabbath School now had 646 scholars and was experiencing timetabling problems. In true Annual Report language, '...the orderly behaviour of the young people' was noted. A Young Men's Sabbath Morning Fellowship Meeting was begun - one hour before the main service- with twenty to twenty-five members and was affiliated to the Glasgow United YMCA. In addition, a class for young men, also affiliated to the GUYMCA, was held on Saturday evenings. The WYMCI report revealed an increase in numbers and interest: 'Mr William A. Smith reports that considerable progress has been made... members have shewn a more active interest in the welfare of the club than ever before.' Classes in History and Geography were added along with a Cricket Club.

The 1883 Report, published in April, of course made no mention of the Boys' Brigade, still to be invented, but some of the personalities of the early Boys' Brigade were already in place. Mr J. R. Hill was helping in the Sabbath School which with 681 scholars simply could not accept any more. A hall at 285 North Woodside Road was taken over as a temporary measure, enabling the school to be divided into Infant, Junior and Senior Sections. The report particularly noted, *'...the increasing number of scholars over the dangerous age of 15 who remain with us.'* It was in fact 142 as against 119 for

Mr. W. A. Smith c.1883

Rev. J. R. Hill

the previous year. Good teaching, good accommodation and a good grading system of infant, junior and senior were seen as the reasons for this success. Here was the challenge for Smith...to keep these young men of 15 plus as a part of the church. The WYMCI, of which Smith was still Secretary, had 59 members and had even started an orchestra!

The Boys' Brigade appeared for the first time in the 1884 Report:

'Thursday Evenings. Boys' Brigade - W. A. Smith & J. R Hill. The Boys' Brigade has been started at the Mission since last year. It is something quite unique in character but extremely interesting, and it already gives good hope of the best results.'

1st Glasgow Company, Boys' Brigade in the Grounds of Garscube 9th April 1885 (The first photograph)

Back row (L-R)

Capt. William A. Smith, Sergt. William H. Wylie, Sergt. John R. Jarvie, Lieut. James R. Hill, Lieut. John B. Hill

Back row of Boys (L-R)

Alexander Fraser, James Wright, William Tunna, William Davidson, Alexander Smith, Gilbert Thomson, John Whitecross, Patrick Kinney, Bandmaster Naughton, L.Corpl. William Stewart, Matthew Collins, Samuel Watson, William Drinnan, Hugh McKenzie, Carl Gillie, William H. Smith, Archibald Fulton.

Middle row of Boys (L-R)

James T. Walker, L.Corpl. George Hamilton, Adam Johnstone, William Tassie, Edward Munro, John Mitchell, John Nelson, John Murray, Daniel McPhee, James Carson, David Aitken, Alexander McFarlane, James Munn, Lewis Lymburn, Hugh Baird, William G. Nelson, Daniel Hay, Donald Davidson.

Front row of Boys (L-R)

Corpl. John Tennant, Alexander Hunter, John Inglis, Charles McLeod, James Wilson, Alexander Junor, Duncan McLean, Andrew McPherson, Jas. Walker, William McCulloch, John Graham, Peter Peddie, L.Corpl. William H. Hendry, Robert Cochrane, George Stewart, Peter Urquhart, Robert T. Randell, L.Corpl. Alexander Dowie.

THE COLLEGE CHURCH—MISSION DISTRICT WORK

Sabbath ..	*Morning*—Fellowship Meeting for Young Men ..	Mr. FINLAY M. ROSS.
	Morning—Boys' Brigade Bible Class	Mr. WM. A. SMITH and Officers.
	Forenoon—Divine Service (11.30)	MISSIONARY.
	After Forenoon Service—Tract Distribution ..	Mr. JOHN WYLIE and others.
	Afternoon— Sabbath Schools (2.30)	*Senior*—Mr. H. M. ARTHUR (Supt.), Mr. J. M. TOMORY (Secy.), and Assistants. *Junior*—Mr. J. A. BALFOUR and Assistants. *Infant*—Mr. E. E. REITH and Assistants.
	Young Women's Class (5 p.m.)	Miss M'LAREN.
	Fellowship Meeting for Young Men (5 p.m.)	Mr. W. A. SMITH.
	Evening (6.30 p.m.)—Evangelistic Service	The MISSIONARY.
Monday ..	*Afternoon*—Mothers' Meeting	Mrs. REITH and Mrs. M'LAREN.
	Evening—Savings Bank	Mr. DONALD MACDONALD and Mr. H. M. PARKER.
	Evening—Library	Mr. JAMES LYALL.
	Evening—North Woodside Girls' Club	Miss MACPHAIL.
	Evening—Young Women's Industrial Meeting ..	Miss BROWN and Assistants.
	Evening—Sewing Class ..	Miss BALFOUR and Assistants.
Tuesday ..	*Evening*—Boys' Brigade Gymnastic Class ..	Mr. GEO. ORR and Mr. P. STEWART.
	Evening—Mission Choir, Lesser Hall	Mr. JOHN WYLIE.
Wednesday	*Evening*—Prayer Meeting ..	The MISSIONARY.
Thursday	*Evening*—Boys' Brigade Drill and Band Practice ..	Mr. W. A. SMITH and Officers.
Friday ..	*Evening*—Band of Hope ..	Mr. JOHN THOMSON.
Saturday..	*Evening*—Gospel Temperance Meeting	Mr. JOHN THOMSON.

Every Week-day *Evening*—Separate Reading and Recreation Rooms for the Young Men's Club, and for the Boys' Brigade.

The object of the BB was stated and the age range for members given as 12 - 17 years. *'In the course of the first three meetings of the Brigade 59 boys enrolled themselves, but the very strict discipline that was introduced had the effect, before many nights were over, of reducing that number by about one half...'* About 30 boys remained until the end of the session and they formed a loyal nucleus from which to build. *'Many of the boys have not missed a single drill from the beginning of the session to the end. There is reason to hope that lasting good has been done to some of them through the agency of the Brigade.'*

Smith had resigned his position as Secretary of the WYMCI by 1885. Sabbath School work was still reported as being, *'...the main feature of our Mission...'*. The Boys' Brigade was said to be a *'great success'* and William Smith reported that the Boys' Brigade had grown, with five other companies in Glasgow and one in Edinburgh. The Mission company, now known as the *'1st*

THE BOY'S BRIGADE.—A COMPANY INSPECTION.

Glasgow' had 55 on the roll which included a Flute Band, started in December 1884, of sixteen performers. The attendance on the Sabbath was obviously working very well as, *'...at the desire of the boys themselves, a Bible-Class was commenced in January last, which meets on Sabbath mornings at half-past nine, and which the boys attend in a way that they would never have done, but for the fact that it is connected to the Brigade.'* Captain Gray, 1st Lanarkshire Rifle Volunteers, inspected the Company on the 19th March, and is quoted as saying: *'The training in*

The Fife Band of the 53rd Glasgow Company Boys' Brigade c.1897- 8 based at the White Memorial United Free Church, Paisley Rd. West, Plantation. The gentleman on the left wearing the kepi is J. Scott Hunter the son of James Hunter, a founder of the Glasgow Foundry Boys' Religious Society. Mr. Scott Hunter, being very musical, was no doubt assisting with the Band.

The Boys' Brigade

Company N°	Member's Name	Address	Rank	Age	Birth-day	1883 October	November
	Wm A. Smith	22 West Mile St.					
	James R. Hill	15 Woodside Quadrant					
1	James Laut	318 North Woodside Road		15	5th Novr		
2	Donald McLellan	9 Garrioch's Rd		15	30th Octr		
3	James Paterson	245 North Woodside Road		15	13th May		
4	Robert Paterson	92 Carriebankie St.		15			
5	John Lawrie	304 North Woodside Road		15	27th July		
6	James Lockhart	117 Henderson St.		15	6th Apl		
7	Alexr Davie	180 Henderson St.		14	4th Mar		
8	Wm H. Wylie	230 North Woodside Road		16	8th June		
9	James Dame	14 Dick St.		13			
10	Wm Black	8 Dick St.		14	11th Apl		
11	Jas Walker	328 North Woodside Road		12	7th Dec.		
12	Jas Murdal	108 Henderson St.		13	8th June		
13	Ed. Hamilton	22 Carriebankie St.		13	25th Aug.		
14	Geo. Hamilton	22 Carriebankie St.		15	2nd Jan.		
15	Wm Lawrie	9 Garrioch Mile Road		12	8th Jan.		
16	Wm Smith	44 Kirkland St.		14	12th Feb.		
17	Wm Sutherland	11 Carriebankie St.		13	25th Aug.		
18	Wm Henna	352 North Woodside Rd		14	20th May		
19	Carl Gielie	17 Garrioch mile Rd		12	17th Novr		
20	Wm Hendry	418 New City Road		13	18th Novr		
21	John Wood	105 Henderson St.		14	14th Aug.		
22	John Service	25 Carriebankie St.		12	18th Octr		

The first page of the original 1st Glasgow Coy Roll Book
NB. Only 'James R. Hill' is listed in this initial register as helping Smith

The Boys' Brigade.

Enrol No.	Members Name	Address	Rank	Age last birthday	Birthday
23	Hugh Baird	318 North Woodside Road		13	3rd Oct 83
24	George Stewart	352 "		11	22nd Dec
25	John Murray	35 Willis St.	12	13	
26	James Barton	39 Dick St.		12	2nd Jan
27	Peter Lyon	105 Henderson St.		13	6th Aug
28	Samuel Morton	19 Moment St.		12	26 Feb
29	George Neil	46 Dick St.		16	19th Oct 83
30	Charles Osborne	230 North Woodside Road		14	15th Dec
31	Alexr Fraser	17 Garriochmill Road		15	27th Aug
32	Wm Hinchaw	11 Carrickanden St.		14	29th Oct
33	George Fulton	26 Raeberry St.		14	6th Oct
34	John Small	25 Willis St.		14	10th Oct
35	James Laidlaw	3 Carrickanden St.		14	29th Dec
36	Alexr Dale	43 Garriochmill Road		13	1st Dec
37	Andrew McPherson	43 Garriochmill Road		14	21st May
38	Patrick Kinney	160 Old Rebbookhill St.		14	30th Jan
39	Wm Wilson	140 Raeberry St.		12	10th Oct
40	Robt Scott	8 Dick St.		13	7th Oct
41	Peter Cameron	31 Park Terrace Lane		12	4th Oct
42	Jno W. McLennan	168 Henderson St.		13	4th Sep
43	Wm Stewart	352 North Woodside Rd		13	4th Sep
44	Hurt McDougall	65 Gardner St.		15	29th Oct
45	Wm Buchan	28 Carrickanden St.		16	10th Nov
46	Joseph Maguire	8 Dick St.		15	29th Jan
47	Thos Philbit	North Woodside Park Limits		14	22nd Sep
48	Arthr Rendell	21 Simpson St.		12	13th Sep
49	John Tennant	124 West Graham St.		15	10th Oct

The second page of the original 1st Glasgow Coy Roll Book

The Boys' Brigade

Company No	Members name	Address	Rank	age last	Birthday	1863 October	November
						4 11 18 25	1 8 15 22 29
50	William Robert Gunn	39 Dick Street		15	24th Jan.	1 1 1	1
51	John Turner	145 Henderson St.		16	14th Oct. 83	1 1 1	1
52	Gordon Caplan	39 Dick St.		15	24th Sep.	1 1 1	1
53	John Murdoch	230 North Woodside Road		16	9th June	1 1	1
54	Hugh Hanna	169 Henderson Street		16	13th Aug.	1 1 1	
55	Daniel Watson	230 North Woodside Road		15	15th Aug.	1 1 1	
56	James Anderson	37 West City Road		15	11th Oct.	1 1	
57	Earnest Bonney	12 Henderson St.		15	16th June	1 1	
58	Lewis Lipschuns	174 Henderson St.		14	17th Dec.	1	
59	Wm Philips	North Woodside flint works		12	14th Apl.		

The third page of the original 1st Glasgow Coy Roll Book

military drill and order cannot fail to instil habits of discipline, obedience, regularity, and politeness, thus fitting the individual members to take and keep their places in the greater battle of life, with its varied temptations and irregularities.'

There were some forty-two companies of The Boys' Brigade by 1886. Smith wrote: *'We began this session with 77 members on the roll, an increase of 22 compared with last year.'* There was much parental support expressed for the drill: *'This military drill, with all its invaluable training and discipline, has been felt and seen to have beneficial results as ever, both in the Sabbath School and in the home life of the boys, the parents being unanimous in their testimony on this latter point.'* Further advances were made by 1887 with 65 companies with 3,000 boys, being operated in Glasgow alone. Smith reported that at the end of the last session a number of the old boys of the company had to resign because they had reached the age limit, but he commented proudly, *'...they all joined the Branch of the Young Men's Christian Association connected with our Mission, while three of the old sergeants are now teachers in our Sabbath School.'* The Company Bible Class on Sunday mornings, according to Smith, had grown in interest and attraction for the boys. Fifty of the boys had spent a week in camp at Tighnabruaich during the Glasgow Fair Holiday and a Cricket Club had been formed as a way of keeping the boys together during the summer months. 1887 was the year the North Woodside Girls' Club was formed. The Girls' Club was an extension of the existing Young Women's Sewing Meeting and the Junior Sewing Class which were now united and including songs and games in the meetings.

The Boys' Brigade had grown so rapidly in strength and popularity that by 1888, according to the Report, *'...it bids fair to take rank as a National Institution.'* William Smith was now devoting all his time to its conservation and development whilst retaining his special connection to the 1st Glasgow. In the Report, the activities of the company were outlined in sections: the Company Bible Class, Military Drill, Band Practice (now with brass instruments), Gymnastic Class, Ambulance Class, Cricket, Football and Swimming Clubs and the newly opened Boys' Room. The Boys' Room was open every night of the week and was opened to prevent the, *'...demoralizing effect upon the boys of hanging about the street corners at night for want of any better place to go.'* Smith concluded his report: *'Boys they are to the backbone, full of all a boy's restlessness and life, and yet eager, in all the work of the Brigade, to conform to those habits of obedience and order which must prove invaluable training for the battle of life.'* Smith's Report for 1889 started thus:

'The little company of 3 Officers and 30 Boys, on which we reported for the first time in the Annual Congregational Report for 1884, has now grown into a regularly constituted organisation, with a permanent Headquarters' Office and Staff, an official "Gazette" and a present strength throughout the United Kingdom of 320 companies, 1050 Officers, and 13,700 Boys, with affiliated branches in the process of formation in New Zealand, Canada and the United States.'

After reporting on all the thriving aspects of company work, from Bible Class to Summer Camp, he summarizes what the BB company was all about:

'In the work of our Company, we seek to provide abundant channels through which the healthy instincts of boy nature may flow to some purpose and some profit; to surround the boys continually with influences that make for goodness and for God; to set a high standard of life before them; and in the words of their Company card, we expect them, wherever they are, 'always to endeavour to maintain the purity, kindliness, courtesy, and mutual confidence that should prevail in a company of Christian boys.'

In 1891, Smith regretted that he had to retire from his post with the Mission Sabbath School owing to the pressure of his BB commitments. Indeed, the BB had grown to become a worldwide organisation. In addition to the 418 companies in the United Kingdom there were now companies in the USA, Canada, Australia, New Zealand, South Africa and elsewhere. The Mission was experiencing a large turnover in its leading personnel, so Smith's leaving of his post was not regarded as significant. Athletics, Football and Swimming had been added to the company programme and were regarded as a , *'...desirable feature of boy-life. In this way it has brought these games under Brigade influence, and has done much to elevate them, and to show, that, if wisely directed, they may be made a valuable training ground, not only for the physical, but for the moral natures of our boys.'*

As part of the introduction to the BB Report of 1892 an interesting, and slightly baffling word of caution was given by the author of the Church Report. *'The Brigade seems now entitled to be recognised as a great accomplished fact, and while every one admits its value as an aid to physical training, the problem with which some are at times exercised is how the movement can be best developed as a great moral and spiritual force.'* It's hard to see how the Brigade could have been doing more. The Bible Class was better attended than in any other year and a joint missionary meeting was held in conjunction with the YMCA where Professor Drummond gave an address. Could it be that the author of the Church Report was giving voice to those who regarded the new Brigade as putting too much emphasis on the military aspect of its existence and too little on the religious? If so, it is interesting that such criticism was very close to Smith who must have known the author. That it was published - and expressed in such vague a manner - may reflect that the congregation was not entirely supportive of Smith's endeavours. Musical Drill with arms had been added to the usual routine of Company Drill. According to Smith's 1895 Report, many of the boys: *'...when they leave the Brigade, become members of the YMCA in our Mission, which are now for the most part composed of old members of the Company, and a large majority of the office-bearers of which are "old-boys" of the 1st Glasgow.'*

The Funeral of Sir William A. Smith
The hearse drawn-up outside the Free College Church
16th May 1914

CHAPTER TEN

The Birth of a Worldwide Movement

The Boys' Brigade was founded as one company of boys in 1883. William Alexander Smith was hoping to solve the problems of inattention and ill discipline in his Sunday school. The fundamental question that needs to be asked is: why was it that Smith's Boys' Brigade went on to become a world-wide youth organisation when its forerunners, particularly the Glasgow Foundry Boys' Religious Society, did not? Smith enthusiasts would say, 'cometh the hour…cometh the man.' and put it down to his undoubted great charisma and leadership skills. Undeniably, Smith was the right man, in the right place at the right time and with the right idea.

Smith was certainly the right man. He was used to standing on his own feet. According to his son, G. Stanley Smith, he would as a youngster, drill the other boys in the old barn of his home, Pennyland House in Thurso.[224] He was still a young boy of just thirteen when he went to live, and eventually work, in the Empire's Second City, far from the remote farmhouse in Caithness. In 1868, after his father died on a business trip to China, young William had been taken-in by his uncle Alexander Fraser, a Glasgow clothing merchant and member of the Free Church. By 1878 Smith had, by studying and working long hours, established himself as part of the business community of Glasgow

by setting up, along with his brother Donald, an exporting company, 'Smith, Smith & Co.'. Smith was very much abreast of the latest business methods and progressive ideas. He was soon to develop and weave together his interests of religion, young people's welfare and soldiering.

From 1874, part-time soldiering as a member of the Volunteers occupied much of his spare time, although certainly not with the approval of his pacifist Free Church uncle Alexander. For Smith, however, it seemed a natural thing to do since his father and grandfather had both been professional military men and his father had even been a major in the Caithness Artillery Volunteers in Thurso following his full-time service in the Dragoon Guards. Involvement in the Volunteer movement, roughly the equivalent of today's Territorial Army, was certainly not unusual for any young Glasgow businessman in the 1870s and '80s. Living in Hillhead, a prosperous part of the West End of Glasgow, it was hardly surprising that he enlisted in the 1st Lanark Rifle Volunteers, very much the unit established for professional men such as he. In December 1881, when Smith resigned due to pressure of business he had risen to the rank of lieutenant, being acknowledged as one of the most popular officers. He re-joined in 1884 reaching the rank of Lieutenant Colonel before retiring in 1908. The title of honorary colonel was retained until his death.

Glasgow was the right place. The Second City of the Empire, it was wealthy, full of churches and newly literate young people. The Church of Scotland had been very much at the centre of the community in Smith's youth and whilst Smith was growing up in Glasgow, under the influence of his uncle, he had been exposed to the teachings of its breakaway, the Free Church. Religious revivals were underway at the time in the city and Smith attended the evangelistic meetings of Americans Moody and Sankey from February 1874. As the up and coming new church in the city and needing new members, the Free Church was keen to encourage all activities associated with youth, so organisa-tions such as the Band of Hope and the YMCA were particularly favoured. Smith had joined the YMCA in 1872 which for him was the first step towards membership of the church. The College Free Church, under the leadership of Rev. George Reith, responded enthusiastically to the meetings of D. L. Moody, and was quick to establish missions within the surrounding densely populated area, including the North Woodside Mission. Reith was certainly a great influ-ence upon William Smith, as biographer William Clow testifies, *'Many of the younger members of his congregation, such as William A Campbell and William Smith, received a fresh baptism, and responded to their young minister's voice and his appeal with a fearless confession.'* [225] Filled with this new zeal, Smith soon became a reg-ular worshiper at his uncle's church, the College Free Church of Scotland in Glasgow's affluent West End, joining as a member in April 1874, the same year he joined the 1st Lanark Rifle Volunteers. [226] The fact that the Boys' Brigade linked itself to these expanding individual churches and their missions was undoubtedly one reason for its extraordinary success.

The time was right, since throughout the century youth work had been growing in importance. There was a culture of religious philanthropy in Scotland in which experiment had been fostered and encouraged. Tremendous support for this embryonic youth work had come from the wealthy 'Dissenting Liberal' families who had given succour to local young men's institutes in the Glasgow area since the 1840s. The Spoutmouth Young Men's Institute, formed by Sir Michael Connal in the East End and his Buchanan Institution in the Calton and Bridgeton area supported by Sir William Collins, who was present at the first BB Public appearance in March 1885. The latter had even introduced Bugle Bands and 'single-stick' drill into its juvenile programmes. The Grove Street Mission Institute founded in 1858, and its 'Foundry Boys Department' was extremely popular, as was William Quarrier, the Baptist who had established his Working Boys' Brigades, including the Shoe-black Brigade in Glasgow in 1865. Like much of the United Kingdom, the Education Acts of the early 1870s were now quite evidently responsible for producing young people versed in the 3 Rs. There was scope, however, for informal, character-building education.

Where, or from whom, did Smith get his idea, his 'model' for a Boys' Brigade? It can be assumed that Smith, during his years in Glasgow from the late 1860s, would have been aware of a number of initiatives designed to steer young people away from the un-christian temptations of the expanding metropolis. One of these early organisations, the Glasgow Foundry Boys' Religious Society (GFBRS), was certainly known to him in the late 1870s after he joined the Volunteers, because a branch met at his local Drill Hall, that of the 1st Lanark Volunteers. The GFBRS had its origins in the iron foundries of the banks of the Clyde. Here, impressionable young boys, sometimes of the tender age of only ten years, were exposed to the coarse and rough manners of the adult moulders and had inevitably adopted their habits. Foundress, Mary Ann Clough, herself a working - class girl had initially made it very much a working - class organisation. Sadly, by 1862 the Foundry Boys organisation had virtually folded due to Mary Clough's emigration to New Zealand. However, it was to be born again in 1865 from the missionary zeal of middle and upper - class nineteenth century Glasgow philanthropists, a section of society in which Smith would play an important part. The newly reformed GFBRS, the one with which Smith would have been familiar, adopted a format much more akin to that of its eventual progeny the Boys' Brigade.

Events in Edinburgh associated with the highly esteemed, well-publicised 'no-popery' abstinence campaigner and keen Volunteer John Hope working in many parts of the city, with his 'British League Cadets' since the 1860s and still active in the 1880s, would certainly have been known to Smith. Smith was present for some of the Volunteer reviews in Edinburgh, such as the 1881 Royal Review, where the British League Cadets always took part. It would have been difficult to miss some two hundred of them in their bright red Garibaldi shirts!

In fact the Colonel of the 1st Lanark Rifles, Lt. Col J. N. Smith, was so impressed with the cadets on parade that the following year he attempted to start a 1st Lanark Cadet Corps: *'Col Smith...threw out a hint that if the parents of young lads gave sufficient encouragement, he was ready to undertake the formation and drill of a Cadet Corps. In order to stimulate the movement, he had on the platform a young lad dressed in the proposed uniform. It was at once neat, useful and inexpensive, but it did not meet with the support expected, and the project was allowed to drop.'* [227] This proposed Cadet Corps came just after William Smith had resigned from the 1st Lanark, but it seems likely that he would have attended the recruiting event or at least known all about it. Rev. Dr. Thomas Guthrie who was a prominent Free Church minister in the City and a keen Sunday school teacher, spent time encouraging the Glasgow Foundry Boys was a supporter of John Hope's endeavours and was generally interested in helping young people. Guthrie's son eventually became National President of The Boys' Brigade. Existing movements such as the YMCA only served young people over the age of seventeen, as recounted by William Wylie, the first BB Sergeant, *'When we reached the manly age of 13 most of us felt that we were too big for the Sunday School and we left it. There was, therefore, a gap of a few years until we were able to join the YMCA at 17, and it was to fill this gap that Captain Smith formed the Boys' Brigade.'* [228] The Band of Hope, which featured strongly in the North Woodside mission's programme, was very much centred upon temperance and abstinence, but it had a simple accoutrement uniform, was organised into groups and included both ceremonial and awards.

The idea - the BB model - was developed as a response to a particular local need. Smith had become involved in the Young Men's Society at the College Free Church from the year he joined in 1874 and had been helped in that enterprise by the Hill brothers - James and John. This eventually led him to be directed into working at the North Woodside Mission Sunday School. Dr Herbert Gray, the assistant minister at the Church said this of him, *'From the very first I was impressed by his amazing capacity for detail ... He was very strict but also very kindly and understanding ... He seldom talked religion, he practised it.'* [229] In his biography of Smith ('Pioneer of Boyhood') [230] Roger Peacock, who knew Smith well, recalled his personality:

'Quiet and unruffled as he was in manner and speech, he was not a man with whom anyone would choose to take liberties. There was a look in those penetrating eyes which could quell a mutiny or tame a tiger - (or a panther!) let alone subdue a bunch of unruly boys! It is certain that any group of boys in his charge were always thoroughly under control. While there was

little of the despot or martinet in his make-up, there was about him an authority and a kindly masterfulness which was a priceless possession for a man whose life was to be devoted to the leadership and training of boys.' (Author's parenthesis)

However, Smith was no miracle-worker and the reality of retaining the older children, particularly those who were teenagers, caused him to think carefully about his methods. The immediate difficulty seemed to arise in simply controlling his charges, particularly the boys, whilst in the Sunday school. Contrary to many modern accounts, the 'boys' were not grubby, bootless little street urchins. They were in fact from very decent homes, well-fed and clothed and many holding down a regular job in an office, factory or shop. To these literate, healthy, youths the very idea of 'Sunday School' was 'old fashioned', since it was aimed at 'wee-bairns' not at 'young men' as they saw themselves - they had been there and done that. They were adolescents who had placed the whole concept of 'school' firmly behind them and were consequently in danger of disassociating themselves from the church altogether. The only reason many of them attended at all was that, *'parents compelled them to do so'*. [231] Parents, it may be assumed, often viewed attendance as a vehicle for upward social mobility, and some employers also expected and encouraged it. Smith was not alone in his concerns. There was much angst amongst the church and civic authorities concerning the perceived 'problem' of this newly recognised, some would say newly created, section of society. Even the Sunday school movement itself was questioning the tenets upon which it had been founded, now that elementary education was compulsory for all. Smith had to search his soul, and perhaps his memories of stories and methods he had heard through his Free Church friends and Volunteer colleagues, for a solution.

The establishment of what eventually became the 1st Glasgow Company of The Boys' Brigade was Smith's response. He had got to know the Mission boys very well, many being the sons of skilled working-class fathers. It was probably this knowledge of the boys, and particularly of their liking for all things military, which took him, in the summer of 1883, along with his colleagues the Hill brothers, to see the Rev. George Reith and the other leaders of the College Free Church to suggest the formation of The Boys' Brigade. If we want a definitive reason for Smith's approach, we can do no better than quote Smith's own words - a rarity - from a speech to the Scottish National Sabbath School Convention at Arbroath on 30th September 1887:

'...What led to the formation of this company was the felt want of something that

would hold and interest the elder boys of the Sabbath school. In this school we had every advantage we could wish, in the way of admirable accommodation, good teachers, and the best of superintendents, and yet in spite of all of these we could not fail to see that we were not solving the question of how to retain and influence our senior boys. The great majority of them left the school about the age of 15, under the evident impression that they were too big and manly for the Sabbath school; and even those we did keep were not turning out the type of young men that we would have desired to see. And so the idea of the Boys' Brigade was conceived and wrought out with a view to overcome both these difficulties; and the experience of four years has shewn that, wisely conducted, it is capable of fulfilling the most sanguine anticipations that had been formed concerning it. It is not only retaining the boys in the Sabbath school, but while doing so, it is being made the means, in God's hands, of moulding their lives and characters for Christ, and encouraging them in every way to take their stand on His side as the noblest and manliest thing a boy can do.

In proceeding to work out the idea of the Brigade, we came to the conclusion that nothing could be so attractive to a boy as some organization of a military nature. Boys are inherently fond of soldiering and drill, and we decided to take hold of this fact and use it for Christ. We often hear the complaint that so few boys are Christians. Is it not possible that, in Christian work among boys, we may have gone too much on the lines of seeking to commend Christianity to them by shewing the boy the same side of it as would commend it to the gentler nature of the girl?' [232]

There is, doubtless, an implied criticism here, by Smith of the way in which the existing Glasgow Foundry Boys' Society had some years before relinquished uniform and introduced girls into all of its activities, as well as the normal Sabbath school organization.

No doubt the experience and confidence with military formalities generated by being a Volunteer himself helped considerably with his suggested formation of a 'brigade'. The object, in his mind, was to start with discipline, proceed with reverence and inculcate the self-respect which seemed to be lacking in 13 to 17 year olds. Frederick P. Gibbon, in his biography of Smith, summed up the need very well:

'The Boys of a Sunday school do not usually develop the team spirit, because the common interest is insufficient. The school meets for an hour each week; the attendance is irregular in the case of the older scholars; and they are listeners only, not active participants. They engage in no form of work or play in which teamwork is called into action.' [233]

The innovation which Smith proposed was to introduce week-night activities and employ a military method. Initially, Sunday classes would remain the same. Smith must have been quite apprehensive about this request, however,

William Smith and the 1st Glasgow NCOs (detail) Session 1898-99

because he knew that some members of the congregation would oppose it on religious grounds. The idea of a military method was certainly not new; it had been phased out by the GFBRS over the previous eighteen years and was now no longer used, partly because of opposition from the churches. In fact, the phasing out of uniforms and the admission of girls from 1870, had taken the GFBRS along a path quite divergent from what eventually proved to be the successful BB model. The GFBRS was, as a Religious Society, still held up as being at the forefront of Sunday school work in Scotland and further afield. So it was perhaps quite deliberate that Smith did not start with any 'uniform' in his Boys' Brigade, choosing to adopt a more acceptable red rosette worn in the button-hole typical of those decorating many Bands of Hope and Sunday School fife bands over the previous twenty-five years. That is how they were presented at their first public Inspection in March 1885. He knew that uniforms and rifles would not be universally popular with members of the Free Church congregation. The very title, 'Brigade' today smacks of militarism, but it was not so in 1883. There had been many examples of working 'brigades': wood-chopping brigade, doorstep brigade, crossing-sweeping brigade and some shoe-black brigades that were not in any way military, or even uniformed. Even in 1910, John Brown Paton, the founding President of the pacifist Boys' Life Brigade replying to a letter from Dr. Scott Lidgett, clearly approves of the name 'Brigade': *'Lastly, I have carefully thought over what you have said about the word 'Brigade'. It commended itself to me, and I must say it still commends itself most strongly, because the word 'brigade' means a company - small or great - of those who unite in a close band for some definite work...'* [234] On the other hand, if Smith had chosen 'cadets' as a name it would have aroused far more dissent from the religious pacifist lobby. To have called it a 'society' would have been in direct open competition with the GFBRS. Perhaps the importance of the name has long been underestimated as one of the reasons for the Brigade's success. Any modern-day advertising executive would soon be out of a job if he adopted the principle that the name of a product was not important.

A halfway-house 'uniform', of accoutrements, along with dummy, wooden rifles was introduced, however, in April 1885 and the first known photograph shows the Company wearing it outside Garscube House early that same month. (see pic . page 120) So what led to this? By 15th October 1885 there were 15 companies, twelve in Glasgow all in the West End and all having some connection with the Volunteer movement. When those first twenty-three boys paraded in the North Woodside Mission on and after 4th October 1883 what was to be their idea of a 'Brigade'? There is no doubting that these original BB boys wanted to drill, just like the army. To them, the nearer 'BB' was to the real thing, the better. According to R. S. Peacock the boys wanted the uniform accoutrements and Smith made them wait more than twelve months in order to have something of a 'carrot' to which the boys could look forward. [235] Did Smith always intend to adopt a military style uniform, or did he initially have concerns that this may be a step too far? He was faced with a delicate balance between the Church's problem - what to offer in order to retain the interest of the older boys - and what would be acceptable to the Church as a solution. Anecdotal evidence from the son of one of the founder members of the 1st Glasgow BB suggests that the boys may have requested Smith to find them a

Sir William A. Smith Inspects ex-members in Liverpool - 1912

'military' style uniform similar to that which had been worn by the Foundry Boys in their parents' day. [J] Some elements of the accoutrement BB 'uniform' probably came from the Volunteers and some from the Foundry Boys. Although the concept of wearing accoutrements over normal clothing is nearer the Foundry Boys model, it is not wholly the case since the Foundry Boys adopted a full tunic uniform for its NCO ranks. The 1st Lanark Volunteers had worn 'pillboxes' between 1872 and 1878 during Smith's first period of service, so perhaps there were, by 1885, some remaining in the quartermaster's stores which became available. The mounted detachment, which Smith commanded

The Gordon Boys' Brigade in Southampton, formed in 1885,
operated a Messenger Brigade and a Shoe-black Brigade

The Church Lads' Brigade, formed in 1891, a highly successful
Anglican clone of The Boys' Brigade became a large international
organization. It united with the Church Girls' Brigade in 1978

after re-joining in 1884, seems to have retained this headgear however, as can be seen on a contemporary photograph. [236] Haversacks only became compulsory in the 1st Lanark Volunteers from May 1885 [237] after a meeting where Smith was present; although they had been 'recommended' since 1862 and used for some years. [238] Clearly, haversacks are being worn by 1st Glasgow BB a month before, on the first photograph taken outside Garscube House. The first parade of 1st Lanark with haversacks was on 8th May 1886 for their field day: *'For the first time the Regiment paraded with haversacks, and that addition to the ordinary uniform gave the men a smart and serviceable appearance.'* [239] Leather accoutrements were supplied to 1st Lanark by Messrs Leckie, Graham & Co. and not surprisingly they became suppliers to The Boys' Brigade.

In the climate of the 1860s and 1870s the only 'Brigade' clothing models were those of the 'charity' clothing worn by shoe-blacks and boys on reformatory ships or that worn by 'cadets' sponsored by rich philanthropic benefactors. The tunic version of the uniform may have been seen as a negative feature by the men in charge of the GFBRS, or even perhaps the boys themselves in those early days, and thus assisted its decline. But what a difference a generation makes. By 1885 any presumed 'stigma' of boys dressing up in uniform accoutrements seems to have completely gone, at least, from the boys' standpoint. This was not the case, however, with some of the Churches. The first Baptist BB Coy, the 3rd Glasgow, associated with the Adelaide Place Baptist Church's St. Clair Street Mission, failed to survive more than a few weeks before it was closed by the Deacon's Court because they couldn't sanction *'...anything that tends to foster a warlike spirit in boys.'* In the case of the Baptist churches it was probably the idea of using model rifles for drill that would have made acceptance of the BB rather difficult. It would certainly not have been simply the uniforms since William Quarrier, the founder of the uniformed Glasgow Industrial Brigades, was associated with Adelaide Place from 1863 and for the rest of his life. [240]

The support of eminent Churchmen such as Professor Henry Drummond, Rev. Dr. Marcus Dods, Rev. Dr. Donald Macleod and Lord Guthrie ameliorated the legitimate concerns of the Church authorities who must have found it difficult to accommodate this 'fighting and praying monster'. Smith actively sought the backing of other nationally known figures such as Lord Shaftesbury the great factory reformer and philanthropist, who had been chairman of the Ragged School Union for 40 years, to both legitimise and popularise the Brigade. In a letter to Shaftesbury at his home in Wimborne Dorset on 3rd July

The Manchester City Mission Brigade operated for more than thirty years after World War Two

1885, enclosing a photograph of the 1st Glasgow Company and a copy of the Object, Smith told the great reformer of the progress made by the Brigade and requested his opinion as to its worth. *'I believe so thoroughly in this work, and feel so intensely interested in it, that I am anxious to avail myself of the influence which your name and experience would carry...'* The Earl, who was ill and in the last weeks of his life, replied via his Secretary stating: *'His Lordship...fully sympa thises with your views, and he believes that Boys' Brigades...would be very useful'* [241]. Speaking at the Scottish National Sabbath School Convention in Glasgow in 1890, in front of such eminent people as Michael Connal and William Quarrier, Rev. Dr. Donald Macleod looked back on the progress made by the Sabbath Schools and other organizations in the city. Firstly, he praised the Board Schools: *'I am thankful for compulsory education, and I am thankful for free education as regards the whole of the subjects that are free, and I am thankful that the Board schools are turning out children to our Sunday schools, where you have not got the enormous trouble of opening evening classes and teaching them to read and write the ABC. Another great improvement is the effect of the discipline of the Board schools getting to the waifs and ragamuffins and little ones that used to kick up rows and break the hearts of the good lady teachers.'* [242] Macleod went on to differentiate between good and bad Sunday schools: *'A good Sunday school is a source of untold benefit, and a bad Sunday school is a source of untold evil. A Sunday school in which the discipline is slack and in which the good-hearted teachers have not the power of*

The Oratory Boys' Brigade was a Roman Catholic Brigade based at the Oratory School in London

producing silence, in which there is a continual struggle going on between teacher and the taught, a threat here and a row there and a clang in this corner, and where they are brought up really learning disorder instead of order, and disobedience instead of obedience, I say that that Sunday school is doing a mighty power of evil instead of good. To see them filling the street with noise when they come out like a set of savages is a most deplorable affair.' [243]
Finally, Macleod addressed the visitors to Glasgow from further afield:

'Those who have come from other parts of the country will find a deal worth studying in Glasgow - not only in Sunday schools, but in some other things. There is one organisation I think almost peculiar to Glasgow - the Foundry Boys' Association - and I think the Convention will find a great deal that is interesting in the Boys' Brigade, which I am glad to hear is flourishing.' [244]

Like all crazes, particularly those involving young people, uniformed religious youth-work modelled on Smith's 'brigade' ideal rapidly established itself throughout society. Brigade organisations included versions for the Anglican Church: The Gordon Boys' Brigade, The Church Lads' Brigade and London Diocesan Church Lads' Brigade. For the Jewish Community - the Jewish Lads' Brigade. For the Roman Catholics - The Catholic Boys' Brigade. For the pacifist dissenting churches - The Boys' Life Brigade, and, for those keen on guns, The Boys' Rifle Brigade. By the end of the century most church denominations had their own specific brigade for boys, from the Unitarians' Boys' Own Brigade to the New Church Society's New Church Boys' Brigade. Even outside the church community the 'Brigade' method continued to be developed into the early twentieth century as the best way of inducting boys into the world of work. Groups having a direct lineage from the Shoe-blacks, such as District Messenger Boys, Telegraph Messengers and Gordon Boys employed the 'brigade' method.[S] Others relating to specific activities, such as the Boys' Naval Brigade, also adopted the system. Even schools, such as the Roslin School in Midlothian, used the 'Brigade' method.[T] Clearly, Brigades were now viewed as the universally accepted method for training the young people of the nation; a youth which less than fifty years before had hardly been recognised.

The Boys' Brigade, from it's earliest days an International movement, (it reached San Francisco, California, before Birmingham, England) has a large presence in many countries. It expanded rapidly in the USA as 'The United Boys' Brigades of America' before declining in the first quarter of the twentieth century. Today there is rapid growth in the far-east, particularly in Hong Kong, Malaysia and Singapore. In many African countries the Boys' Brigade and Church Lads' & Church Girls' Brigade, adopt methods which would not have been out of place in mid-19th century Britain. Poor children, often with very little schooling, are being re-directed, sometimes from begging on the streets, and are taught life-skills including earning a livelihood, for

The Boys' Life Brigade was a pacifist organisation founded in 1899 by the National Sunday School Union. It united with The Boys' Brigade in 1926

example in farming. Cash is raised in many ways to build schools. One Cameroon company operates a wood-chopping service, selling bundles of firewood. [245] Just like the Shoe-blacks of the 1850s in Britain the uniformed youngsters are seen to be improving themselves, and they are supported by the wider community.

The Better Britain Brigade, operated in Anglican Missions between 1916 and 1945

The Jewish Lads' Brigade, formed in 1895 with the motto 'They go from strength to strength'. It united with the Jewish Girls' Brigade in 1974

Post Office Telegraph Messengers at Drill c.1910

The London Diocesan Church Lads' Brigade, formed in 1891 as a parallel organisation to the CLB. The two brigades worked together from 1918 and united formally in 1936

The Catholic Boys' Brigade, founded in 1896, had a motto of
'Ne Cede Malis' (Don't give-in to evil)

London 'District Messenger' Boys at their Annual Camp

The United Boys' Brigades of America, formed in 1894 to bring together the various American Boys' Brigade organizations

The FDF (Frivilligt Drenge-Forbund) The Danish Boys' Brigade - began in 1902 in a Copenhagen suburb similar to Glasgow's Hillhead following the Founder, Holger Tornoe, reading a work by Henry Drummond.

WALSALL BOYS' RIFLE BRIGADE.

HEAD-QUARTERS :—

WALSALL COMMERCIAL COLLEGE,

BIRMINGHAM ROAD.

COLONEL COMMANDANT :—

LIEUTENANT-COLONEL H. JOHNSON

(Late Captain Royal Lancashire Fusiliers).

OBJECT.

The elevation of the Moral, Physical, and Spiritual Welfare of its Members, and everything that tends towards the promotion of Obedience, Self-respect, and True Christian Manliness.

THERE ARE A FEW VACANCIES

IN THE

VARIOUS COMPANIES OF THE WALSALL BATTALION

Respectable Boys desirous of Joining should apply to the Sergeant-Major ; or to any of the Sergeant-Instructors, at Head-quarters, on Thursday Evenings.

Application can also be made to the following at any time :

CALDMORE.—Colour-Sergeant Wilson, 30, Caldmore Road ; Colour-Sergeant Burt, 33, Caldmore Road ; Sergeant Alexander Davis, 40, West Bromwich Road ; Corporal Harold Machin, 36, Arundel Street ; Corporal B. Hallewell, 40, Arundel Street.
BRIDGEMAN STREET.—Colour-Sergeant Poole, 54, Queen Street ; Bandsman Proffitt, 176, Queen Street.
PLECK.—Sergeant Ernest Jackson, 48, Prince Street ; Corporal Herbert Price, 21, South Street ; Bandsman Herbert Whitehouse, 101, Wednesbury Road.
HATHERTON STREET.— Sergeant Abram Davis, 129, Hatherton Street.
STAFFORD STREET.—Colour-Sergeant Coley, 108, Stafford Street.
BRIDGE WARD.—Sergeant Toon, White Swan Inn, Dudley Street ; Corporal George Tandy, 13, New Street.

The Walsall Boys' Rifle Brigade accepted 'Respectable boys' aged between 10 years and 17 years. Drills were on Thursday evenings at 6.30 p.m. and Saturday afternoons at 3.00 p.m..

The Trinity Hall Lads' Brigade, Henley-On-Thames. Camping in the 1920s

CHAPTER ELEVEN

Summary and Conclusion

Socially, Britain in the late eighteen hundreds was quite different from that of the middle years of the century. That new post-Crimean War 'Volunteer' age was fearful of imperial defeat and foreign invasion. Combined with an increasing virulently xenophobic, often anti-democratic, quasi-totalitarian, militaristic and Social Darwinist 'national efficiency' movement, it created a totally different intellectual and emotional environment in which new kinds of brigades for boys were born and nurtured. A hundred years later, U.S. President, J. F. Kennedy's famous Inaugural Address of 20th January 1961, epitomised the sentiment. *'And so, my fellow Americans: ask not what your country can do for you - ask what you can do for your country.'* In the 1880s, what the country could do for destitute or lower working class 'rescued' youth by the provision of such necessities as filling stomachs and full employment was no longer at the forefront of philanthropic provision. Elementary schooling was now provided by the state, although education was still regarded as appropriate and suitably uplifting for those who had left behind them at the age of thirteen the offerings of the national systems. Provision of food, work, education, recreation and the issue of pseudo-militaristic uniform, in the paternalistic 'top down' approach adopted in the early part of the century, was now needed to a much lesser degree. In fact, the young recipients of benevolence, such as the Shoe-black Brigades were decreasing in number, and those remaining probably resented being singled out in this way. Shoe-blacks and other rescue societies were declining in size and diversifying in function. The bright red 'charity' jackets worn by the Liverpool Caxton Brigade, for instance, were replaced with sober blue suits in 1886.[246] The new brigades such as The Boys' Brigade and in particular The Church Lads' Brigade, began to emphasise what the nation's youth could do for their country - economically, and eventually militarily, in addition to the obvious personal improvement to be gained from membership. In fact, by the early twentieth century, remaining 'Industrial' brigades, often carried on identical activities to those of the newer brigades and sometimes even put on joint displays. In 1908 the year that the Minister for War, (Lord Haldane) formalised what young people could do for the nation by launching the Territorial Cadet Association, the Annual Inspection took place of the 34th London Company of The Boys' Brigade, based at Gray's Yard Mission, James St, Oxford Street, W. London, then in its 19th year. Its programme featured two items from the boys of the Central (Reds) Shoe-black Society - an Indian Clubs Display and Bar Bell Exercises with Figure Marching.[247]

The Boys' Brigade and its clones, (the Church Lads' Brigade, Catholic Boys' Brigade, Jewish Lads' Brigade and Boys' Life Brigade) became the beneficiaries

of wealthy patricians whose rôle had changed over the century from being direct donors, or even street-workers, into facilitators. Factory owners, shipping magnates, press barons, and their like, now in greater number than ever as the country became wealthier, continued to step forward to meet the demand. They were happy to do so since they saw direct economic benefits for themselves as employers. Christian religious evangelism, social control and militaristic gains for the country were also high on the agenda. Christian Militarism was gaining favour, epitomised by the formation of the Salvation Army in 1878 and enshrined in Hymns such as *'Onward Christian Soldiers'*, *'Fight the Good Fight'* and

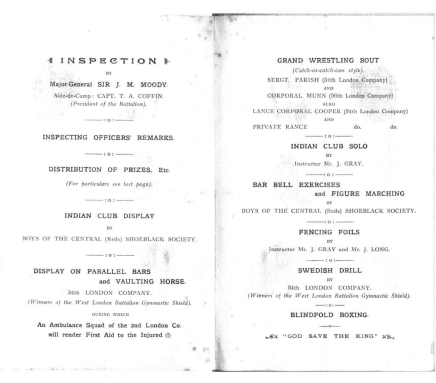

'Soldiers of Christ Arise'. Christian 'Martyrs', such as General Gordon who met his death in 1885, made the idea of 'Muscular Christianity' very much more fashionable than it had been when promulgated by the likes of 'Rob Roy' MacGregor earlier in the mid -19th century. In the formal education sector and in institutions such as residential homes, the three decades before the 1880s had experienced a gradual moving away from the 'military' approach towards a more domestic family environment. (This is exactly what had happened in the GFBRS and with Quarrier's Homes). 'Education' which had followed the concept of 'training for a job', usually a 'traditional craft' industry such as shoe-making, tailoring, blacksmith or carpenter, etc. was also changing. Factories, offices and communication industries wanted employees who would be educated generally and be part of a team, the latter such as post and telegraph, railways, trams etc. were usually uniformed positions. The expanding British Empire required soldiers and sailors in greater numbers than ever before. Generally, supporters of the Brigades were sponsoring opportunities for working youths' newly acquired 'free' time in evenings and weekends. Such leisure time had previously been the sole preserve of a very small section of privileged upper-middle and upper-class boys who attended the public schools. Now being part of a team with an 'esprit de corps' was seen as being not only desirable, but also readily accessible to all. In the last two decades of the 19th century many of the early Brigades were now almost unrecognisable from their origins just forty or so years earlier, but the new brigades, with their voluntary 'semi-military training' were taking over.

The emergence of the Boys' Brigade was part of an evolutionary process and not the revolution it is often hailed to be. The Brigade movement could be said, however, to have come of age with the formation of The Boys' Brigade. The new organisation certainly embodied much that had gone before whilst seeking to address the particular conditions of the mid - 1880s. Male teenagers were on the streets only in the evenings and at weekends instead of every day. These youngsters, generally better fed, clothed and educated, were still a potential threat to society, but now it was for a different reason. The problem of juvenile delinquency was a major problem even at the end of the century. Russell and Rigby in their pivotal work of 1908, concerned themselves with the problem of the 'ike', the 'hooligan' and the 'peaky blinder' terms used in Manchester, London and Birmingham respectively for street boys not ashamed of prison.[248] Russell and Rigby quoted *'Studies of Boy Life in our Cities - 1904'*, edited by Edward Johns Urwick, for the Toynbee Trust, who calculated that in London alone there were at least a hundred thousand boys, *'In whose lives a good club or brigade would make a difference.'* [249]

The emphasis upon Scottish organisations as progenitors of the Boys' Brigade and its offspring is quite deliberate. The Boys' Brigade was born in Scotland within the context of a religious and philanthropic culture. Sunday Schools and Institutes broadened their remit as soon as Board schools took over the basics of formal education, replacing the 3Rs with character-building activities and life-skills. Much of the early philanthropy stemmed from religious conviction and, in the context of the perceived threat of foreign invasion, accepted and approved of sections of its male youth being attired in pseudo-militaristic uniform, both for its own good as well as that of society. Whilst differences of approach could certainly be found between the 'Covenanting' church in western Scotland and those in the east, the essential ingredients were clearly in place well before 1883.

Central to this work has been an examination of the gradual progression and development of Brigade type organisations during the 19th century. For the first time charting that development and the discovery of critical indicators of change has been achieved. Problems still arise, however, as regards the causative factors influential in explaining such changes. It is difficult to identify a single significant factor which triggered the brigade boom, but a combination. National and international transport and communication was so much better in the late nineteenth century than it had been just a single generation before, word of successful brigades spread rapidly and there were many international brigade ambassadors such as Prof. Drummond. Missionaries took the brigade idea with them when they sailed to Africa, Asia and Australasia. There was a greater access to printed materials and a boy population which was now, as a result of being at school for longer, able to read and to understand more about their world. Young shop-workers, apprentices and delivery boys soon got to find out about their British Empire army heroes in publications such as the 'Boys' Own Paper' and the stories of G. A. Henty and, like most boys, wished to emulate them. The Brigades responded to an immediate pressing need to provide something constructive, re-creative and spiritually uplifting for the newly literate sons of the aspirant upwardly mobile skilled artisan and lower-middle class families which had young men with time on their hands. The growth of larger better-fed families outgrowing their relatively small apartments and houses provided a 'push' factor which got the young people out of the home for many hours on most evenings. Socially there was a growing recognition of 'youth' as a distinctive period in the development of young people between childhood and adulthood. The failure of the Sunday school, and the 'Institute' movements to cope with older boys had not been fully addressed, so the real alter native presented by the brigades was taken up widely. The spiritual renewal and evangelism called for initially by individuals such as Moody and Sankey in the 1870s, inspired preachers to look to the young and leaders to volunteer. Consequently, the development of extensive new Church and Mission premises provided the perfect venues for brigade meetings, particularly as the new brigades were almost totally church and denomination based and not reliant upon rented halls. In Scotland, and in many other part of the UK, a response was required to the widespread abuse of alcohol and the brigades were seen as a natural partner for the 'Bands of Hope' or the Junior Rechabites. Some brigades, such as the Boys' Rifle Brigade, would seem to be a culmination of efforts made in Britain throughout the nineteenth century to inculcate a means of social control following on from the mid nineteenth century initiatives to prevent the growth of Chartism, anarchy and Republicanism. The various strands are so intricately and densely woven that it has proved impossible to determine only one common root or origin.

What is certain is that the appearance of The Boys' Brigade represented a significant step forward in the provision of uniformed youth-work. It was the first 'modern' uniformed youth organisation in the same way as some say that the Great War was the first 'modern' war. But like that war, it was not the first.

The Roslin School Brigade c.1910 with the girls. Note the initials 'RPS' in the caps. (Roslin Public School)

NOTES, REFERENCES
and
PHOTOGRAPH
Acknowledgements

NOTES

A. Uniformed brigades founded in 1885 in tribute to and as a memorial for General Gordon. Sponsored by funds subscribed in memory of the late military and philanthropic hero, they operated in a number of places in Britain, notably, Liverpool, Nottingham, Southampton, Dover and Portsmouth.

B. Various 'House Boys' Brigades' existed from the 1870s. In the 1880s these were often run in conjunction with the Gordon Boys Societies, such as in Nottingham. House Boys operated from headquarters buildings which generally included residential accommodation. (See Chapter 5)[250]

C. The Boy Scout Association (1908), The Incorporated Church Scout Patrols (1909) and The British Boy Scouts (1909).

D. In her book *'Philanthropy in Victorian Scotland'*, [251] Olive Checkland makes a clear distinction between the initiatives of the middle classes largely in the interests of their own kind, and the efforts made to assist working classes. She sees the army (Volunteer force) as influencing the Sunday school movement in the formation of the Glasgow Foundry Boys followed directly by the Boys' Brigade. On the other hand she explains that it was the missions which led the way in reaching the poor working class. This would seem to over simplify the whole complex network of influences as well as denying the humble origins of the Foundry Boys, born into a mission environment.

E. Founded c.1860.

F. Quarrier appealed for the establishment of a Shoe-black Brigade in Glasgow similar to the one in London [252] This was launched shortly afterwards.

G. All were either founders, or supporters of Shoeblack Brigades.

H. A founder of the Glasgow Foundry Boys' Religious Society 1865.

I. In 1911 the Church Lads' Brigade affiliated to the Territorial Cadet Force. It was followed by The Jewish Lads' Brigade and Catholic Boys' Brigade. Many units of the Boys' Brigade were also Cadets after 1917.

J. Anecdotal evidence (obtained in July 2001, by interview) from Charles McCulloch, grandson of William McCulloch of 164 Henderson Street, who joined the original 1st Glasgow Boys' Brigade company in 1884, and appears on the 1885 Garscube photograph, (page 120) suggests that it may well have been the boys themselves, and not Smith, who pushed for the introduction of uniform. Uniform was only introduced some 18 months after the foundation of the BB. The Glasgow Foundry Boys' Religious Society had given up the use of uniform and much of its military drill, in some cases as much as thirteen years before, and was not initially keen for its members to join the BB.[253] Some of the earliest BB recruits, like William, who had lost his father in a Gas Explosion in January 1881, were members of the Foundry Boys Society but evidently attracted by the militaristic method, particularly the drill, when he joined. The concept of uniform and drill being 'suffered' because it meant access to other perceived benefits fits with the early and mid 19th century 'charity' model rather than that of the late 19th century when drill became the attraction. The McCulloch's were very much a 'BB Family', with William's four sons, Robert, Charles, James and William being members of the 114th Glasgow at Henry Drummond Memorial Church in Ardoch St.. Grandson Charles [son of Charles Snr.] was a member of the 154th Glasgow at Langlands Congregational Church and Elderpark Parish Church (Amalgamated around 1950).

K. Whilst at the Manchester City Mission MacGill encouraged the development of Institutes such as Grove Street. One of the most famous, the Heyrod Street Institute in Ancoats supported as part of its work a very famous Lads' Club run by C. E. B. Russell (co- author of 'Working Lads' Clubs') in 1908 when the club had some 602 active members, only one of whom was a Shoeblack.[254] The Club held its first meeting on March 7th 1889. In the Autumn of 1893, not long after Mr. Russell had arrived at the Club, it was decided to start a company of The Boys' Brigade, the 5th Manchester. Russell was appointed Captain because he had experience in the Dulwich College Cadet Corps and the East Lancashire Volunteers.[255] Membership of the BB became compulsory for all lads under 17 years attending the club. In 1908, there was still a need for him to run a *'Destitute Lads and Discharged Prisoners' Aid Department'.* [256] C. E. B. Russell served on the Executive of the BB from 1894 - 1906 and was appointed H.M. Chief Inspector of Reformatories and Industrial Schools in 1913.

L. The Glasgow Foundry Boys' Religious Society
In 2007 the headquarters of the GFBRS moved to be co-located within its only remaining branch, the Garngad Branch at the Glasgow Foundry Boys Church,

15 Tharsis Street Glasgow G21. Between 1973 and 1988 the 155th Glasgow Company of The Boys' Brigade operated at that church, underlining the close relationship between the two organisations. Whilst the Tharsis Street Church is owned by the Society, this was not normally the case with most branches meeting, as they had always done, in churches, Institutes and other public buildings. In the early 1990s six smaller branches of the Society, mainly on housing estates, were handed over to the Crusaders Society. The last summer camps, held at Pittenween Fife, also continued until the early 1990s.[257]

M. In complete contrast, some 100 years later the architecture of the new 'Albermarle' youth clubs would directly oppose those of the Grove Street pattern of 'Divide and Rule', large, open, social - mixing areas being regarded as essential.

N. The original Boys' Brigade anchor was based on that used by William Smith's family and was nothing like the one used after 1885.[258]

O. Wording on Sinclair Monument, from direct observation by the authors August 1999 and September 2008.

P. An ancestral relative, Robin Sinclair, Viscount Thurso, was President of the Boys' Brigade between 1985 and 1995.

Q. Sir John George Tollemache Sinclair Bart. Catherine's nephew, lived in Thurso Castle and was evidently a supporter of the volunteers. In October 1861 he reviewed the Artillery and Rifle Volunteers along with the Earl and Countess of Caithness. The Edinburgh Evening Courant of the 23rd October [259] re-printed an extract from the John o'Groat Journal which reported that the Volunteers: *'...under the command of Captain Smith...marched to a park in front of Pennyland.'* It is almost certain that the 'Captain Smith' mentioned here was William A. Smith's father. It is quite possible that Catherine Sinclair was present and almost certainly seven year old William would have watched everything happening right in front of his home.

R. Walter Gee, the founder of the CLB, retained his interest in Temperance and was no doubt, very pleased that, on Thursday December 7th 1893, the first branch of the Church of England Temperance Society affiliated to the CLB was his own Pioneer Company at St. Andrew's Fulham. The account of the evening is given in the very first edition of 'The Brigade' for April 1894: [260]

'...The Company was drawn up at open order, and received the Colonel (Twynham) with the general salute, when he inspected the ranks. Mr W. M. Gee, the Captain, then put the Company through some drill, and was much complimented by the inspecting officer on the smartness and bearing of the Company ... Mr Gee then asked those who wished to join to sign the pledge. It had previously been impressed upon the lads that they should think well before signing, and that it was no light undertaking. It was now getting late, so when thirty-one had signed, the lads were told that the rest must do so another time. "Caps Off" and prayers were then said, and the Company was dismissed. Thus, unostentatiously, in the modest "headquarters" of the Company over a stable, was inaugurated a work which we hope and believe will be far-reaching in its effect on the lives of the manhood of the future.'

S. The Gordon Boys' Home in Stepney, actually ran a company of the London Diocesan Church Lads' Brigade, one of the first 31 LDCLB companies to be registered. Details are listed in the First Annual Report of the London Diocesan Council for the Welfare of Young Men (1892), Lambeth Palace Library. The 'full' (tunic), Gordon Boys' uniforms used by other units were very similar to the LDCLB design. At Dr. Barnardo's in Stepney Causeway a 'Brigade' uniform was worn by the Messenger and Shoe-black Brigades based there.

T. Since 1891, at the Public school (Elementary) in Roslin, Midlothian, the Headmaster, Mr White, had encouraged the older boys to stay on. One method was the use of drill. The Dalkeith Advertiser of 27th July 1894 reported that White was concerned because he knew that the boys who left at 11 or 12 years of age *'...ran wild before getting regular employment'*. Other Midlothian schools, such as Lasswade, were also using military drill and had been doing so since 1888. The Senior School Board Officer, A. V. Brown was fully supportive even acting as Drill Officer in some of his schools! Mr Andrew Mochrie a veteran of Crimea was the regular 'Drill Instructor' at Roslin. In 1897, the boys paraded in unifoms and with carbines very similar to those of The Boys' Brigade. Reported in local press: *'The boys of Standards III and VI presented a very smart appearance in their neat forage caps and waist belts.'* [261] Similar reports continue for the next thirteen years. (See picture page 156)

X. In 2009 the private journal of Mr Henry Alfred Offer the manager of the Castle St. Working Boys' Home, 15, Hanover Street, Long Acre W.C. 1867 - 1872, was offered for sale through Jarndyce the London Antiquarian bookseller. The published description of the contents included the opening by Quintin Hogg on 15th June 1867 and the fact that a Shoe-black Society was formed along with a 'Crossing Sweeping Brigade' by James Weave.

REFERENCES

CHAPTER 1
Introduction

1. Cox, J. (1982) *The English Churches in Secular Society* Oxford. O.U.P.
2. Checkland, Olive, (1980) *Philanthropy in Victorian Scotland. Social Welfare and the Voluntary principle.* Edinburgh, John Donald.
3. Army Cadet Force Association (1982) *The Cadet Story 1860 - 1980.* London. A.C.F.A.
4. Collins, L. J. (2001) *Cadets - The Impact of War on the Cadet Movement.* Oldham, Jade Publishing.
5. ibid. p.7.
6. ibid. p.2.
7. Glasgow City Mission (1827) *First Report* Glasgow University Library.
8. ibid. (1832) *Sixth Report*
9. Lord Provost, *Letter to the (1829) ...on the Expediency of a House of Refuge for Juvenile Offenders,* 2nd April. Glasgow, Mitchell Library,
10. (1953) *Boys' Brigade in Kirkcaldy, The, from its beginnings to the present time* May, Allen Litho Co Ltd, Kirkcaldy. (R. Bolton Collection)
11. Daily Courant, The (1860) *12th March, 20th March, 24th May.* Edinburgh, Central Library.
12. Volunteer Review (1860) May, *The Cadet Corps of the London Rifle Volunteer Brigade* London, Imperial War Museum.
13. Scotsman, The (1860) *31st August p.2.* Edinburgh, National Library of Scotland.
14. Scotsman, The (1861) *21st November p.4.* ibid
15. Boys Own Magazine (1862) *Jan, Vol. 1 No. 1,* London, Imperial War Museum.
16. Westlake, R.(1982) *The Rifle Volunteers.* Chippenham. Picton Publishing
17. Murdoch L, (2006) *Imagined Orphans. Poor Families, Child Welfare, and Contested Citizenship in London.* New Brunswick, New Jersey and London, Rutgers University Press.
18. ibid. p.122
19. ibid. pp. 122 & 134 quoting: Chadwick, Edwin (1859) *The Military and Naval Drill; with Systematised Gymnastics as part of National Education.* National Association for the Promotion of Social Science, Education Section,Bradford, 2, Papers of Sir Edwin Chadwick, 92. University College London Archives.
20. Birmingham Saturday Evening Post. (1858) *The Saint Martin's Shoe Black Brigade.* Birmingham Central Library
21. Arkinstall, P, & Bolton, R, (2002) *Forward! The Birmingham Battalion of The Boys' Brigade 1902 - 2002* Little Aston, RB Publishing.
22. Springhall, John et.al. (1983) *Sure & Stedfast - A History of The Boys' Brigade,* London & Glasgow, Collins

23. Spriggs - Smith W.J., Rev. (c1904) Leaflet: *The Knights of Peace Protest against the Military Spirit encouraged by The Boys' and Lads' Brigades*. CLCGB Archive Collection, Wath-upon-Dearne.

24. Horn, Pamela (1997) *The Victorian Town Child p.221. Appendix 1*, Stroud, Sutton Publishing.

25. Drummond, A. L. & Bulloch, J. (1975) *The Church in Victorian Scotland, 1843 - 1874, p.2* Edinburgh.

CHAPTER 2
Glasgow Sunday Schools and Institutes

26. Glasgow Sabbath School Union Annual Reports. *(1841, 1851, 1861, 1871,1881, 1882, 1883, 1884, 1886, 1888, 1889, 1890.)* Glasgow, University Library.

27. Gillespie, Andrew, (1898) *Sir Michael Connal and his Young Men's Institute, A Story of Fifty Years,* Glasgow, Morison Brothers. Glasgow, Mitchell Library.

28. Ragged School Work (1886) *Our Ragged School and How it Became an Institute, Report of a meeting of Ragged School Teachers Held in the City Mission Rooms Sat. March 13th p.11.* J. Wakefield MacGill, Manchester City Mission. Edinburgh, National Library of Scotland

29. Self Help (1866) A Magazine for Working People. *p.6.* Edinburgh, National Library of Scotland.

30. Gillespie Op.cit. *p.104*

31. ibid. *p.129*

32. ibid. *p.51*

33. Booton, Frank, (1985) Editor, *Studies In Social Education, Vol 1: Work with Youth 1860 - 1890, 1, Youth Clubs and Institutes, Arthur Sweatman 1863. pp. 40 - 49* Benfield Press, Sussex.

34. Springhall J., et al Op.cit *p.36.*

35. Connal, M. (1835-1893) [1895] *Diary of Sir Michael Connal,* Glasgow, Mitchell Library.

36. Wallace, J (1995) *A Mission to Glasgow's Urban Poor, A Case Study of the origins of the Grove Institute with lessons for today. p.3.* Dissertation HON 402 Glasgow Bible College. [Now International Christian College]

37. Evangelistic Work (1868) *A record of the operations of the Grove Street Institute, Glasgow.* Edinburgh, National Library of Scotland.

38. Ragged School Work. Op.cit. *p.11.*

39. Wallace, J. Op cit. *p.6.*

40. Ragged School Work. Op cit *p.21*

41. ibid. *p.36*

42. ibid. *p.37*

43. Grove Street Home Mission Institute, (1877) *18th Annual Report.* Glasgow, University Library.

44. ibid. *p.17*
45. Ragged School Work op. cit *p.36*
46. ibid.

CHAPTER 3
Ragged/Industrial Schools

47. Montague C. J. (1904) *Sixty Years in Waifdom, or The Ragged School Movement in English History. p.33* London, Chas Murray & Co, Reprint, (1969) London Woburn Press.
48. London City Mission (1840) *Fifth Annual Report, p.16 Quoted in Montague C.J. p.34.*
49. Harris, David (1867) *An Industrial Brigade as an adjunct to the Ragged Schools in Edinburgh.* Open letter, 27/09/67, Edinburgh Public Library.
50. Dickens, Charles (1852) *Charles Dickens on Ragged Schooling* from The Daily News 13th March, reproduced in www.infed.org/archives. 2001-
51. Healey, Edna (1978) *Lady Unknown, The Life of Angela Burdett-Coutts* Sidgwick & Jackson, London
52. ibid.
53. Edinburgh Original Ragged School *(1848, 1850, 1855, 1859, 1861, 1862, 1874,) Reports* Edinburgh, National Library of Scotland, & *(1878, 1880, 1883,1884, 1886, 1887, 1888, 1890,1892, 1893, 1894, 1895, 1899, 1900) Reports* Edinburgh, National Archives of Scotland.
54. Mackie, Peter (1988) *The United Industrial School of Edinburgh - A Bold Experiment* Innes Review Vol 39 No.2 Edinburgh Public Library
55. United Industrial School, The, (1851) *A Sketch of its Origins, Progress and Practical Influence. pp. 23-25* Edinburgh Public Library.
56. ibid. p.27
57. United Industrial School, The (1848 - 1890) *Annual Reports,* Edinburgh Public Library.
58. ibid.
59. Howie, Les, (2006) *George Watson's College - An Illustrated History. p.331* Edinburgh, George Watson's College.
60. Montague C. J. op. cit. *p.400*
61. Scotsman, The (1861) op.cit. *8/8/ p.3*

CHAPTER 4
The Glasgow Foundry Boys' Religious Society

62. Checkland Olive, op.cit. *p. 54.*
63. Ragged School Work. op.cit. *p.21.*
64. Checkland Olive, op.cit. *p. 55*
65. Self Help op. cit. *p.13*
66. Gordon, W. J., (1888) February 4th, *The Problem of the Poor, The Glasgow Foundry Boys* in The Sunday at Home - A Family Magazine, pp. 74 - 77. Religious Tract Society, London. (R. Bolton Collection)
67. ibid. *p.75.*
68. Glasgow Foundry Boys' Religious Society (1965) *And In the Beginning,* Centenary booklet, Edinburgh.
69. ibid.
70. Self Help op. cit.
71. Glasgow Foundry Boys' Religious Society (1867) *First Annual Report, p.9* Glasgow, Mitchell Library
72. Glasgow Foundry Boys' Religious Society (1965) op.cit
73. Springhall J, et. al. op.cit *p.37*
74. Fraser, Brian, (1981) *Origins and Early History of The Boys' Brigade, p.84.* Doctoral Thesis, Glasgow, University of Strathclyde.
75. Glasgow Foundry Boys' Religious Society (1881) *Fifteenth Annual Report, p.16.* Glasgow, Mitchell Library.
76. Glasgow Foundry Boys' Religious Society (1867) op. cit.
77. ibid.
78. Glasgow Herald, The (1866) *21st July Glasgow Foundry Boys' Religious Society - Fair Week Excursion to Inverary. p.26.* Appendix to First Annual Report GFBRS, Glasgow, Mitchell Library.
79. Elliot, Mary (1979) *Short History of the Glasgow Foundry Boys' Religious Society* - A 45 min. talk - typed copy. (R. Bolton Collection)
80. Checkland Olive, op.cit. *p.56*
81. Glasgow Foundry Boys' Religious Society. (1881) op.cit. *p.9 & p.22*
82. Springhall J, et. al. op.cit *p.37.*
83. ibid. *p.41*
84. Foundry Boy, The (1886) March, *Magazine of the Wellington Palace Branch,* Glasgow, Mitchell Library
85. ibid. *May*
86. ibid.
87. Foundry Boy, The (1886) op.cit. *May.*
88. Springhall J, et. al. op.cit. *p.37*
89. Glasgow Foundry Boys Religious Society (1925) *Diamond Jubilee, 1865 - 1925, p.31-32* Edinburgh. National Library of Scotland
90. Glasgow Foundry Boys' Religious Society (1870) *Psalms and Hymns Selected for the Sabbath Forenoon Services and Week Evening Evangelistic Meetings.* J. McCallum Glasgow. Edinburgh, New College Library.
91. Foundry Boy, The (1886) *May.* op.cit.
92. Scott Hunter, James (1953) Extract from the *'Foundry Boy in Action Magazine'* Nov.

1953 *Open letter to G. Stanley Smith, Esq. MBE, MC Brigade Sec. The Boys' Brigade, London.* (Photocopy, R. Bolton Collection)

CHAPTER 5
Shoe-blacks, Industrial Brigades and Training Ships

93. MacGregor, John (1882) *The Story of the Shoeblack Brigade* in January, Home Words for Hearth & Heart, London, Home Words. (R. Bolton Collection)
94. Fireside, The, Pictorial Annual (1892) Edited by Rev Charles Bullock BD, *The Story of 'Rob Roy' and his canoe p.124* & Series of articles. London, Home Words Publishing Office. (R. Bolton Collection)
95. MacGregor, John. op.cit.
96. Fireside, The, op.cit. *p.124.*
97. Leapman, Michael (2001)*The World for a Shilling, How the Great Exhibition of 1851 Shaped a Nation. p.108.* London, Headline.
98. Edinburgh Evening Courant (1864) 4/1 *What the Shoeblacks Make* quoted from London, Churchman's Family Magazine. Edinburgh, National Library of Scotland.
99. Hogg, Ethel M. (1906) *Quintin Hogg, A Biography,* London, Archibald Constable.
100. Hodder, Edwin (1895) *John MacGregor 'Rob Roy' (3 ed.). Chapter 4. p.86.* London, Hodder Brothers.
101. Winter, James, (1993) *London's Teeming Streets 1830 -1914, p.138,* Routledge, London & New York.
102. S.C. (Select Committee) (1852) on *Criminal & Destitute Juveniles, Vol 7 q. 3457 .*
103. Winter, James, op.cit. p.141
104. Lennox, Cuthbert (1901) *Henry Drummond A Biographical Sketch pp. 204 -205* Andrew Melrose, London
105. Winter, James, op.cit. *p.141.*
106. *Ragged School Union Magazine* (1851) *Vol 3, pp. 68-9* (Quoted in Montague C.J. 1904)
107. Hodder, Edwin. op.cit *p.88*
108. Montague, C. J. op.cit *p.199*
109. MacGregor, John. op.cit.
110. Times, The (3/8/1863) *p. 6.*
111. Montague, C. J. op.cit. *p.196*
112. ibid. *p.197*
113. Low Orr, Robert, Sherrif, (c1923) *Lord Guthrie A Memoir. p.206* London, Hodder & Stoughton.
114. West London Shoeblack Society (1885 - 1902) *Minute Book. Bessborough Place, Pimlico. 1885 - 1902.* London, Library of Westminster Chapel,Buckingham Gate.
115. Christian Worker, The (1886) *Volume VII, p.119,* Published in connection with the

Manchester and Salford Boys' and Girls' Refuges and Children's Aid Society, Cassell & Company, London E.C. (R. Bolton Collection)

116. ibid. *p.91.*

117. ibid. *p.122*

118. ibid. *p.138*

119. Leslie, Marion (1909) The Kensington House Boys' Brigade. A Novel Parish Organization, in Home Words pp. 110 -112, London, Home Words Publishing Office (Photocopy-R. Bolton Collection)

120. ibid.

121. Times, The (1882) *Inquests* p.10 Issue 30641 ColF (Times On-Line)

122. *Letter from J.Kirby, Manager of Pimlico House-Boy Brigade (*1910) April 26th in www.hiddenlives.org.uk/caseimages.

123. Harris, David, op.cit.

124. Gordon, W. J. (1888) April 7th, *The Problem of the Poor, The Edinburgh Industrial Brigade,* in The Sunday at Home - A Family Magazine pp 219 - 221, Religious Tract Society, London. (R. Bolton Collection)

125. Harris David, (1902) *'Preventative Service' - In memory of William Rattray, 33 years Superintendent of the Edinburgh Industrial Brigade Home.'* Edinburgh, Public Library.

126. Ross, James (1971) *The Power I Pledge, Being a Centenary Study of the Life of William Quarrier. pp 35-38.* Quarrier's Homes. Glasgow

127. Urquhart, The Rev. John, (c.1901) *The Life-Story of William Quarrier, pp 67 - 69* S. W. Partridge & Co. London.

128. Evans, B (2002) *The Training Ships of Liverpool, p.33* Birkenhead, Countyvise Ltd.

129. Bolton, R, Howie, L and Mandry, R, (2000) *Badges of the Brigade Vol 1 The Boys' Brigade. p.8.* Little Aston, RB Publishing.

130. Evans, B op.cit *p.109*

131. *Brigade Magazine, The (1894) October, & Executive Minute Book No 2 p.183, January 1895,* Archives of The Church Lads' & Church Girls' Brigade, Wath-upon-Dearne, S. Yorkshire.

132. Evans, B op.cit *p.5*

133. ibid. *p.11*

134. ibid. *p.33*

135. Ross, James op.cit. *p.53*

136. Montague, C.J. op.cit. *pp. 230 - 231*

137. Higginbotham, Peter (2009) *The Workhouse* Web-site www.workhouse.org.uk

138. Times, The, (10/1871) Quoted in *Forest Gate School District Annual Reports of Managers* (1888) 7, FGSD 19, London Metropolitan Archives.

139. Arkinstall, P & Bolton R, op.cit. *p.80*

CHAPTER 6
Edinburgh Pioneers -
Catherine Sinclair and John Hope

140. Hall, S. C. (1871) *A Book of Memories of Great Men and Women of the Age. From Personal Acquaintance* London. National Library of Scotland.

141. Parker, William Mathie, (1967) *Catherine Sinclair,* Published in the Edinburgh Tatler No.73 May. *Scrapbook of Press-cuttings etc.,* (c1800 - 1864) Edinburgh Public Library.

142. Edinburgh Evening News, (1882) *18/09. Scrapbook*: ibid.

143. Edinburgh Evening Courant, (1860) *07/09.* N.L.S.

144. Sinclair, Catherine, (1861) *Letter Undated, but W/B 21/04/61(To Prof. Blackie)* Mss 2643 f.170-171 N.L.S.

145. Edinburgh Evening Courant, (1861) *27/04,* N.L.S.

146. Barclay, J. B. (1985) *Pill Box and Service Cap, The History of Edinburgh Battalion The Boys' Brigade, Edinburgh,* The Boys' Brigade, Edinburgh Battalion.

147. Sinclair, Archdeacon (c1864) [attributed]. *Brief Tribute to Catherine Sinclair,* Scrapbook: op.cit.

148. Sinclair, Catherine, (1861) *Letter undated, but probably October. (To Prof Blackie)* Mss 2643 ff 162-75 N.L.S.

149. Edinburgh Evening Courant (1861) *14/12 'The Sinclair Volunteers'* N.L.S.

150. Parker, William Mathie, op.cit.

151. Jamie, Rev David, (1907) *John Hope, Philanthropist & Reformer. p.13* Edinburgh, The Hope Trust.

152. Scottish Record Office (1859-1893) *John Hope. Papers, Pamphlets, Press Cuttings* GD 253/226/24. Edinburgh.

153. ibid. GD 253/226/6 & GD 253/226/8.

154. Scotsman, The, (1857) *01/04 p.4* Scotsman Internet Archive Site

155. Scottish Record Office, op.cit. GD 253/181

156. Jamie, Rev David op.cit. *p. 183*

157. Scottish Record Office, op.cit GD 253/226/25

158. ibid.

159. ibid. GD253/226/26

160. Scotsman, The (1861) *20/08 p.2* Scotsman Internet Archive Site

161. Scottish Record Office, op.cit GD 253/47

162. Jamie, Rev David op.cit *p.185*

163. Scottish Record Office, op.cit GD 253/47

164. ibid.

165. Scotsman, The, (1861) *20/08 p.2* op.cit

166. Scottish Record Office, op.cit. GD 253 226/27

167. ibid. GD 253/226/30

168. Scottish Record Office, (1862) op.cit. GD 253/60 *Letter from Geo. Wedderburn,* 25 Ainslie Place.

169. Westlake, R. op.cit. *p.45*

CHAPTER 7
Temperance and Teetotal

170. Campbell, Richardson (1911) *Rechabite History, p.156* Manchester. National Library of Scotland

171. King, Elspeth, (1979) *Scotland Sober and Free. The Temperance Movement, 1829 - 1979*, Glasgow Museums and Art Galleries, Edinburgh, Public Library

172. ibid. *p.7*

173. ibid.

174. *Temperance Reformation in Scotland, The, (1929) with Special Reference to John Dunlop and Greenock 1829 -1929, p.26* Greenock. Edinburgh, National Library of Scotland.

175. ibid. *p.33*

176. Morris, Edward (1855) *The History of the Temperance and Teetotal Societies in Glasgow. Chapter 12.* Glasgow, Mitchell Library

177. *Scottish Temperance Review,* (1847) Organ of the Temperance League, Edinburgh. National Library of Scotland.

178. *Advisor, The,* (1849) July, Scottish Temperance League, Edinburgh, National Library of Scotland.

179. Morris, Edward op.cit

180. *Advisor, The,* (1849) October, op.cit

181. *Scottish Temperance Review,* (1849) op.cit.

182. ibid. (1850)

183. ibid. (1851)

184. Temperance Congress, The (1862) London. *The Influence of the Band of Hope* Thomas Bowick, Kenilworth. *p.101* Glasgow University Library.

185. ibid.

186. ibid.

187. Springhall, J. et al. op.cit *p.35*

188. Scottish Temperance League, The (1872) *28th Annual Report, Glasgow. pp. 8-9* Glasgow University Library.

189. National Temperance League, *The (1884) Annual.* Edinburgh, National Library of Scotland.

190. Gee, Walter Mallock, (c.1890) *The Nation's Hope, A Practical Text Book for Band of Hope Workers and all interested in the Education and Control of Children, pp.109 - 114*, C.E.T.S., Westminster SW. (R. Bolton Collection)

191. Springhall, J. et al. op.cit *p.23*

192. Campbell, Richardson op.cit

193. ibid.

194. King, Elspeth op.cit *p.14*

195. Campbell, Richardson op.cit.

196. Independent Order of Rechabites (1885) *Jubilee Record,* Exeter 1885. Edinburgh, National Library of Scotland.

197. ibid.
198. *Rechabite & Temperance Magazine,* The (1874). Edinburgh, National Library of Scotland.
199. Cambell Richardson op cit & Springhall J, et. al. op.cit *p.258*
200. Wightman, William (c1900) *The Order of the Sons of Temperance,* Photocopy, n.d., Edinburgh, National Library of Scotland.
201. ibid.
202. Ragged School Work, op.cit. *p.30*
203. Springhall J, et. al. op.cit *p.32*

CHAPTER 8
Young Men's Christian Association

204. YMCA, Glasgow (1866 - 1867) *Annual Report,* Glasgow, University Library.
205. Binfield, Clyde (1994) *George Williams in Context. A Portrait of the founder of the YMCA. p.58* Sheffield, Sheffield Academic Press
206. Auld, James (1897) *Historical Sketch of the YMCA & Fellowship Unions of Scotland (Annual Report)* Edinburgh, National Archives of Scotland.
207. King, Robert (?) *The contribution of YMCA Glasgow to Community Education during the years 1956 to the present.* Dissertation quoted on official Glasgow YMCA web site. The History of YMCA Glasgow 2009
208. ibid.
209. Binfield, Clyde op.cit. *p.39*
210. ibid. *p.11*
211. ibid. *p.17*
212. ibid.
213. Auld, James op.cit
214. YMCA, Scottish National Council (1878) *Annual Reports,* Edinburgh, National Archive of Scotland.
215. ibid. *1879*
216. ibid. *1880*
217. ibid. *1884*
218. ibid. *1885*
219. ibid. *1890*
220. ibid. *1892*
221. ibid. *1893*
222. ibid. *1894*

CHAPTER 9
The Free College Church Glasgow 1877 - 1895

223. Free College Church, (1877, 1878, 1879, 1880, 1881, 1882, 1883, 1884, 1885, 1887, 1890, 1891) *Annual Reports* Edinburgh, National Archives of Scotland

----

CHAPTER 10
The Birth of a Worldwide Movement

224. Stedfast Mag (1954) January *p.1 My Father by The Brigade Secretary G. Stanley Smith OBE MC* Stedfast Publishers, Bletchley, Bucks. (R. Bolton Collection)
225. Clow, Rev W. M. (1928) *Dr George Reith: A Scottish Ministry, p.101* Hodder and Stoughton London
226. Howie, David (1887) *History of the 1st Lanark Rifle Volunteers, p.240* Glasgow, David Robertson & Co.
227. ibid. *p.165*
228. Stedfast Mag op.cit *p.3 The Two Surviving Original Members talk to Stedfast Magazine - 'William Wylie'.*
229. Springhall J, et. al. op.cit. *p.39*
230. Peacock, Roger S (1954) *Pioneer of Boyhood, pp.23-24* The Boys' Brigade. Reprinted 1985.
231. Clow, Rev W. M. op.cit *p.136*
232. Smith, William A, (1887) *The Boys' Brigade, p.1*, Paper read at Scottish National Sabbath School Convention at Arbroath, 30th September 1887. Reprinted from the Sabbath School Magazine for December 1887. (R. Bolton Collection)
233. Gibbon F. P. (1933) *William A Smith of The Boys' Brigade, p.33* London & Glasgow, Collins' Clear-Type Press.
234. Paton, John Lewis, (1914) *John Brown Paton, A Biography by his son, p.434* London et. al. Hodder and Stoughton.
235. Peacock, Roger S op.cit. *p.47*
236. Springhall J, et.al. op.cit. *p.34*
237. 1st Lanark Rifles, (1868 -1924) *Regimental Committee Minute Book,* Edinburgh Castle, United Services Museum Library.
238. 1st Lanark Rifles, (1862) *Regimental Scrapbook:* Q Company: M.1993.771.7: 17.8.1883 Edinburgh Castle, United Services Museum Library.
239. Howie, David op. cit. *p.119*
240. Ross, James op.cit. *p.29*

241. Smith, W. A. (1885) *Letter Book* April 1885 - August 1886, The Boys' Brigade Archives, Felden Lodge, Hemel Hempstead, Herts. HP3 0BL
242. Sabbath School Convention, The (1890) *23rd Scottish National, Glasgow, p.16* Mitchell Library.
243. ibid. *p.17*
244. ibid. *p.18*
245. Botting, Rob & Cowden, Stephen (2006) *Visit to Cameroun* in The Boys' Brigade Gazette *Vol. 114 No 4 October p.129*

CHAPTER 11
Summary and Conclusion

246. *Christian Worker,* The, op.cit *p.80*
247. Boys' Brigade, The 34th London Company. (1908) *Programme of Annual Inspection and Display,* Friday May 22nd (R. Bolton Collection)
248. Russell, Charles E. B. and Rigby, Lilian M, (1908) *Working Lads' Clubs, p.24* London, Macmillan and Co.
249. ibid. *p.27*

NOTES

250. Leslie, Marion (1909) *The Kensington House Boys' Brigade - A Novel Parish Organization,* in 'Home Words' *p.110 - 112,* London Home Words Publishing.
251. Checkland, Olive op.cit. Chapter 3
252. Glasgow Herald op.cit. (1864) *20/11*
253. Springhall J, et.al op.cit. *p.37*
254. Russell, Charles E. B. and Rigby, Lilian M, op.cit *p.390*
255. *Heyrod Street Lads' Club and the 5th Manchester Company The Boys' Brigade, A History* (1910) privately printed by the Committee. p.11, [Sec F. P Gibbon] (R. Bolton Collection)
256. Russell, Charles E. B. and Rigby, Lilian M, op.cit *pp. 406-407*
257. Wallace, J (2009) Pastor of the Foundry Boys Church, *Letter to L. Howie,* March
258. Bolton, R, Howie, L. and Mandry R. op.cit
259. Edinburgh Evening Courant. op.cit (1861) *23/10*
260. Brigade Magazine, The op.cit. (1894) *April*
261. Dalkeith Advertizer, The (1897) 5th August. Midlothian Council Local Studies Library.

PHOTOGRAPHS/ILLUSTRATIONS
Acknowledgements

Front Cover

Cover: Ragamuffin - Website *'Victorian London'* (Lee Jackson) Used with permission, no original attribution available.
A Foundry Boy of the 1860s GFBRS Glasgow

P.v Drawings from: *'Good Words'* magazine 1891. 1891 Isbister and Company Limited, Covent Garden, London. *pp. 96 - 99*

Chapter 1

P. 6 'Just Enough': *The Sunday at Home Family Magazine, For Sabbath Reading,* 1888 *p.305* The Religious Tract Society, Paternoster Row, London. R. Bolton Collection

Chapter 2

P. 14 Sir Michael Connal: *'Sir Michael Connal and his Young Men's Institute, a Story of Fifty Years'*, Glasgow, Morison Brothers. Mitchell Library, Glasgow.
P. 17 The Spoutmouth in the 1860s. ibid.
P. 19 The Band - Buchanan Institute 1913
P. 21 Grove Street Mission Institute Heading. *'Evangelistic Work (1868) A record of the operations of the Grove Street Institute, Glasgow.'* Edinburgh, National Library of Scotland.
P. 24 Grove Street Mission Plan. ibid.
P. 26 The Grove Street Institute in 1895. Heatherbank Museum of Social Work

Chapter 3

P. 29 RSU Magazine Cover *'Sixty Years in Waifdom or The Ragged School Movement in English History.'* C. J. Montague. Chas. Murray & Co. London 1904. Reprinted by The Woburn Press, London 1969. *p.57*
P. 30 The scene inside a Ragged School: ibid. *p.75*
P. 31 Boys on the 'Chichester' ibid. *p.315*
P. 31 Baroness Burdett-Coutts ibid. *p.314*
P. 33 The Ragged School Tree ibid. *p.271*
P. 35 Vagrant Children: *'Street Arabs and gutter snipes, the pathetic and humorous side of young vagabond life in the great cities; with records of work for their reclamation',* 1884, George Carter Needham. Toronto Univ. Library
P. 38 The Brompton Boys' Institute Band. R. Bolton Collection

Chapter 4

Chapter 5

P. 75 Akbar and HMS Conway. *'The Training Ships of Liverpool'*, Bob Evans, 2002, *p.4* Countryvise Limted, Birkenhead. Reproduced with permission.

Chapter 6

P. 78 Catherine Sinclair's Gothic Monument. R. Bolton

P. 79 The Sinclair Fountain in Princes Street

P. 80 Portraits of Catherine Sinclair. In the 1860s - R. Bolton Collection.

P. 82 Young Street, Edinburgh in 2008. R. Bolton

P. 83 The Volunteer Review Medal of 1860: © The Trustees of the National Museums of Scotland. Reproduced with permission.

P. 86 An ironic juxtaposition. Les Howie

P. 87 Catherine's House in George Street and St John's Church taken in 2008. R. Bolton.

P. 88 J. Hope Portrait *'John Hope Philanthropist & Reformer'* 1907, The Hope Trust frontispiece.

P. 89 British League Bible Class 1866. ibid. *p.172*

P. 90 Officers and NCOs No 16 Company Edinburgh Rifle Volunteers 1866 ibid. *p.179*

P. 95 Uniforms of the British League Cadets. Ibid. *p.185*

P. 96 Badge of the BL From The British League Prize List 1865-1866

P. 97 Mr George McGibbon and the British League Office 53 Rose St. The Hope Trust op.cit. *p. 218*

Chapter 7

P. 105 Edinburgh Castle - R. Bolton Collection

P. 108 Brough Boys Temperance Band - R. Bolton Collection

P. 108 Chorley Band of Hope Union Band - R. Bolton Collection

Chapter 8

P. 110 George Williams Founder of the YMCA. *'George Williams in Context'*, Clyde Binfield. 1994, Sheffield Academic Press in association with YMCA England.

P. 114 A very early YMCA-BB medal, awarded by Myers & Marble June 13th 1885. Medal held in private collection.

Chapter 9

P. 116 Rev. George Reith, *'Dr George Reith: A Scottish Ministry'*, 1928, Rev. W. M. Clow, Hodder and Stoughton Ltd. London *p.113*

P. 117 The North Woodside Mission - R. Bolton Collection

P. 119 Mr W.A. Smith c.1883 The Boys' Brigade

P. 119 Rev. J. R. Hill The Boys' Brigade

P. 120 The first photograph of The Boys' Brigade 1885. The Boys' Brigade

The authors wish to thank the many people who have helped with reserach for this book and apologise to anyone not individually acknowledged.
The following are particularly thanked for their assistance:

Dorothy Loudon - Isle of Skye
David Aubrey QC - Llanfaches. S. Wales.
John Cooper - Glasgow
Dr. Brian Fraser - Glasgow
Leslie Hodgson - Edinburgh
Charles McCulloch - Glasgow
Bob Mandry - London
Jack Wallace - Glasgow